Morning Manna

WISDOM SERVED WITH HUMOR AND HEART

T. FAYE GRIFFIN

MOONSTONE
ENTERPRISES

Published by Moonstone Enterprises
Los Angeles, California, U.S.A.

Cataloging-in Publication Data is on file with the Library of Congress.

ISBN 978-0-9905258-0-6

For information write to:
T. Faye Griffin
P.O. Box 352154
Los Angeles, CA 90035
www.morningmannathebook.com

Book Design: DesignsDoneNow.com

Printed in the United States of America
10 9 8 7 6 5 4 3 2 1

For Jo
You never stopped believing.

Menu

HEART HEALTHY MENU
(WHAT THE DOCTOR ORDERED)

SIDE ORDERS
(JUST A LITTLE SOMETHING EXTRA)

LATE NIGHT MENU
(DEFINITELY NOT THE KIDS MENU)

SEASONAL FAVORITES
(GREAT ANY TIME OF YEAR)

Introduction
WHAT IS MORNING MANNA?

Okay, so this whole thing started with a Facebook status update. It was a bright but uncommonly chilly morn here in sunny Southern California. I'd spent a deliciously deep time conversing with the Lord in prayer before preparing for the workday. While making my bed, I decided to listen to a few songs that appeared on my Facebook timeline. One song in particular caught my ear. It was by one of my favorite R&B balladeers, Phil Perry. While not a household name of Bieber proportion, he's one of those amazing unsung artists that have managed to develop a large and devoted following without creating mass hysteria in the media. Phil Perry does things with that honey-dipped tenor of his that can curl your toes and get a rise out of some other choice spots in the anatomy.

Hence my problem.

Between the fluffing of pillows and tucking of sheets I began to feel an...oh let's just call it a little "spark of interest" in my nether regions. For most folks this is not a cause for concern. But as an unmarried person in a committed relationship with Jesus Christ every alarm in my body and spirit went off.

Now don't get it twisted, the Lord is not against sex. He invented it. He created our bodies with all of its various components. He even included an owner's manual to show us how to properly operate them. But you know how we do when we get that box of furniture home from Ikea; we toss the instructions aside and commence building shelves by our own wits. Inevitably, we end up with $200 worth of pressed wood leaning in a corner like the Tower of Pisa. Then we wonder why glue is everywhere and the books keep sliding off. I'll tell you why. Because we didn't read the manual! When it comes to sex and other important life issues Christians face, we often choose to ignore the instruction manual, and end up in a sticky mess with our lives falling apart all around us.

That's my testimony in a nutshell. I'm a devout follower of Jesus Christ who strives to live kingdom principles in a very dark world. As such I experience the same joys and pains, temptations and trials as anyone, including wanting to feel a bit of thunder down under from time to time. How-in-so-ever, I have decided to remain celibate until I get married or until Jesus comes—whichever happens first. (Come quickly Lord Jesus!)

So that morning, as Phil Perry crooned and my hormones hit the fan, I had a choice to make: Either I would continue listening to the sensual lyrics and allow my mind to lose the battle with my body. Or I would shut it all down before it was too late. I elected the latter. I killed the audio (Sorry, Phil) and turned my focus to Facebook. I quickly jotted down this status update:

Note to Self: Refrain from listening to Phil Perry first thing in the morning until you get a husband. Frustration is not a good look.

The response to that tongue-in-cheek post was immediate and intense. People chimed in with a refreshing candor. Fellow singles, Christian and otherwise, (even a few married folks), openly shared how they deal with their personal power surges. Together we laughed, we vented, we related, and more importantly, we prayed.

It was an epiphanic moment. Suddenly, I realized that in the 30-plus years since my divorce my life as an unmarried Christian had inspired many "notes to self" on a great number of topics ranging from parenting to money to friendships. There were notes written in journals, in the margins of my Bible, on napkins, magazine covers, church bulletins and scores of other scraps of paper. Some were the result of some foolishness or nonsense I'd allowed myself to get into that required the grace of God to get me out of. Some were observations from the scriptures that prevented me from "going there." Others were simply encouragements from the Father to let me know that I was on track. Each one was a practical life lesson that most anyone could apply whether single or married.

So I thought if this many people were motivated to relate to one another, encourage one another, or feel less alone in whatever struggle they had as a result of reading one simple truth from my life, then perhaps they may find value in an online devotional filled with them.

I began rising before dawn each weekday to pray, study, and write. God spoke loud and clear to my spirit in those morning sessions. Five days a week he provided a fresh word for me to share with readers. I likened it to the account found in Exodus 16 that tells of the wandering Israelites. They were starving and God, in his mercy, poured down fresh "bread from heaven" from the sky each morning to feed them. They called it "manna." (Exodus 16:4,12,31)

And that's how *Morning Manna* with T. Faye" was born!

The Facebook page caught on quickly. People from around the world joined me at my virtual kitchen table to partake of the wisdom God prepared each day. Soon *Morning Manna* was moved to a WordPress blog site. Before long my beloved readers, whom I call "Diners," made it clear—They wanted a book containing these bites of Biblical wisdom (and they didn't want to have to wait!)

Truthfully, I struggled with whether or not to wait until I had 365 lessons to share. I told God that I didn't want to go out into the marketplace looking crazy. He said, "Too late." Like many devotionals, *Morning Manna* contain brief life lessons, suggested prayers, related quotes and scripture references, but that's pretty much where the similarities end. It's not a daily read.

You can read it in one sitting or put it down and come back to it whenever you like. Also what's different is the subject matter and tone of the book. It's written in the manner of which God speaks to me. Many of our conversations are very casual, even comical; others not so much. Some conversations are brief, others are much longer. Suffice it to say, this is definitely NOT yo' Mama's devotional.

The most important thing to know up front is that book you hold in your hands is presented with a transparency that may be unsettling for some. The goal of the book is to tickle the funny bone NOT the ear. No punches are pulled. *Morning Manna* is also intended to touch and transform your heart. As I mentioned, a lot of what you'll read here comes from my personal journals and therefore is very candid. But you can rest assured that while the book itself may not be perfect, the truth it contains is.

Good, bad, or indifferent I've done my best to present you with clear and concise commentary that can help you gain new levels of wisdom and understanding. Not every subject covered will apply to your life. So, as I always tell the diners, eat the meat and spit out the bones. Are you ready? Welcome to the kitchen table. Your *Morning Manna* is served.

Bon Appetit!

STARTERS

But He answered and said, "It is written,

'Man shall not live by bread alone, but by every

word that proceeds from the mouth of God"

[Matthew 4: 4]

Self-employed? Telecommuter? Unemployed? A word to the wise: Beware of TV time snatchers. It's so easy to get caught up in *The View, The Chew, The Talk, Dr. Phil*, Steve, Ellen, Kelly and Michael and 'nem. But you'll never succeed sitting around all day watching successful people talk about their success.

CHEW ON THIS:

In all labor there is profit, But idle chatter leads only to poverty. [**Proverbs 14:23**]

God,

They say, "a closed mouth don't get fed." Thank you for reminding me that the same goes for idle hands— they don't get paid! I repent for being triflin'.

—Amen

G ot a funky attitude? Well, here's a spiritual Tic-Tac for you:

Everywhere you go you should leave behind the aroma of God.

People should be able to detect His presence through yours. Study His character qualities carefully and work hard to emulate them. Be patient and kind to others (whether they deserve it or not). Stop allowing your funky attitude to stink up the joint. There's enough stank in the world already. (Yes I said, "stank.")

CHEW ON THIS:
Now thanks be to God who always leads us in triumph in Christ, and through us diffuses the fragrance of His knowledge in every place. [2 Corinthians 2:14]

God,
Forgive me for allowing my moods to swing me instead of the other way around.
—Amen

Did you know that it's possible to ban worry from your life? Here's how:

Be
Anxious for
Nothing

CHEW ON THIS:

Be anxious for nothing, but in everything by prayer and supplication, with thanksgiving, let your requests be made known to God; and the peace of God, which surpasses all understanding, will guard your hearts and minds through Christ Jesus. [**Philippians 4:6**]

God,
I've allowed worry to take over the master controls of my mind. But starting right now, I give "the Master" control. Thank you for you peace.
—Amen

Ladies, if God had intended for women to chase men, we would have been born with a rifle and box of buckshot. For Heaven's sake STOP IT! Look, if you catch what you had to chase down you'll have to cage it to keep it, and a man in a cage spends every waking hour thinking of ways to escape. Hunting season is over, Elmer Fudd. Go home and pray that your "prey" will come a'huntin' for you!

CHEW ON THIS:

Charm is deceitful and beauty is passing, But a woman who fears the Lord, she shall be praised. [**Proverbs 31:30**]

God,
I thank you that the man you've created for me comes equipped with an internal GPS programmed to track and locate me no matter my latitude, longitude or attitude.
—Amen

Life can be a big bully. Sometimes it just hauls off and slaps you to sleep then dares you to dream. But it's time to stand up to life. Be bold! Dare to try again. Wake up and DREAM!

CHEW ON THIS:

*"And it shall come to pass afterward
That I will pour out My Spirit on all flesh;
Your sons and your daughters shall prophesy,
Your old men shall dream dreams,
Your young men shall see visions..."*

[Joel 2:28]

God,
You are the giver of dreams. Please restore the ones that have been stolen from me.
—Amen

A re you cheating on God? Have you found yourself a "Part-Time Lover?" Does your attitude and actions have God singing, "Where is the love you said was mine all mine til the end of time?" If so, it's time to get "Reunited." Try re-reading his "Love Letter" to you. It'll touch your heart. Do it so the two of you can once again be "Solid (As a Rock)."

CHEW ON THIS:

Adulterers and adulteresses! Do you not know that friendship with the world is enmity with God? Whoever therefore wants to be a friend of the world makes himself an enemy of God. [James 4:4]

God,
I confess that I've been untrue.
I've hurt your heart and
I apologize. I want to come home
to you. Please take me back.
—Amen

There used to be a bar-b-que joint in Los Angeles with the slogan, "You need no teef to eat our beef." Well, truth is, you need no teef to backbite either—just your tongue. Check the words that are coming out of your mouth. Are they tasty or tasteless?

CHEW ON THIS:

Pleasant words are like a honeycomb; Sweetness to the soul and health to the bones. [**Proverbs 16:24**]

God,
Next time before I open my mouth, remind me to actually listen to the words that come out of it.
—Amen

Thinking about your problems too much? Get out of your own head and get into His. I mean think about it. It couldn't be any worse, could it? Who knows? He may just have some suggestions on how to solve your problem. Could happen.

CHEW ON THIS:

"For My thoughts are not your thoughts, nor my ways your ways," says the Lord. "For as the heavens are higher than the earth, So are my ways higher than your ways, And My thoughts than your thoughts." [Isaiah 55:8-9]

God,
Sorry. You go first.
—Amen

You wouldn't buy a long-sleeved shirt from a salesman with no arms would you? So why are dating someone with no integrity? You're worthy of a loyal, honest relationship. Let go of that character and hold out for someone with character.

CHEW ON THIS:

Do not be unequally yoked together with unbelievers. For what fellowship has righteousness with lawlessness? And what communion has light with darkness?
[2 Corinthians 6:14]

God,
Misery loves company.
Can you help him/her find somebody else to kick it with because I'm out! Thank you for the courage to bounce.
—Amen

Catching a beat-down from your conscience because of that thing you did? Feeling guilty because you "knew better," but did it anyway? Listen, salvation does not mean automatic deliverance from stupidity. Fortunately, God has the awesome ability to take our mistakes and mold them into maturity—if we let Him. So put down that lickin' stick and stop punishing yourself. Time to get up so you can GROW UP!

CHEW ON THIS:

He who covers his sins will not prosper, But whoever confesses and forsakes them will have mercy. [**Proverbs 28:13**]

God,

I've fallen short of your expectations. But now I've turned away from that thing and put it far behind me. So please, restore me. Strengthen me. Grow me. And use me to bring You glory.

—Amen

Faith is when you step out into the imperfect and allow God to perfect it. If he has given you something to accomplish, quit waiting for the planets to align. GO! MOVE! DO IT! He's got your back!

CHEW ON THIS:

The Lord will perfect that which concerns me; Your mercy, O Lord, endures forever; Do not forsake the works of Your hands.
[Psalm 138:8]

God,
I'm activating my faith,
putting my trust in you,
and stepping out into the
invisible net of your will.
Here I go! Wheeeeeeee!
—Amen

Whether you believe it or not, your life has love written all over it. It's written in indelible, blood red "ink" that cannot be washed away. But this "ink" can blot out the stains of your past and rewrite your future with words like: hope, peace, and forgiveness. In fact, let's not call the ink "blood red," let's call it "love red."

CHEW ON THIS:

But God demonstrates His own love toward us, in that while we were still sinners, Christ died for us. [**Romans 5:8**]

Lord Jesus,
I simply want to say, "Thank you."
—Amen

I t is possible to have a steak and potato marriage even on those Cap'n Crunch days. Unconditional love, loyalty and mutual respect can make any relationship taste better.

CHEW ON THIS:

Nevertheless let each one of you in particular so love his own wife as himself, and let the wife see that she respects her husband. [Ephesians 5:33]

God,
I thank you for my marriage. Please help us to always see one another through the prism of your eyes.
—Amen

Don't get mad at the bill collector when he calls your house if you're the one who chose to live the champagne life on a Crystal Light budget.

CHEW ON THIS:

The rich rules over the poor, and the borrower is servant to the lender.
[Proverbs 22:7]

God,

I've been a poor steward with what you've placed in my hand. Please show me how to make a dollar out of this 15¢. Then teach me how to give, save and invest it wisely.

—Amen

A wise woman knows that with God the world is her playground, but without Him she will just get played.

CHEW ON THIS:
A gracious woman retains honor...
[Proverbs 11:16]

God,
May I always be a lady of grace; representing you with my conduct and in my character. —Amen

He says, "I know your works: you are neither cold nor hot. Would that you were either cold or hot! So, because you are lukewarm, and neither hot nor cold, I will spit you out of my mouth." (Revelation 3:15-16)

So the question is: Does your life leave a bad taste in God's mouth?

CHEW ON THIS:

Not everyone who says to Me, 'Lord, Lord,' shall enter the kingdom of heaven, but he who does the will of My Father in heaven.
[Matthew 7:21]

God,
I pray that I come to know you,
not just know about you, so that
my life is sweet to your taste
and a joy to your heart.
—Amen

I t's impossible to be a disciple without discipline. Daily prayer. Daily study. Daily worship. Don't just talk about it. Be about it. BOOM! And God drops the mic!

CHEW ON THIS:

Then He said to them all, "If anyone desires to come after Me, let him deny himself, and take up his cross daily, and follow Me. **[Luke 9:23]**

God,
I confess that I've been talkin' the talk and not walkin' the walk. Forgive me for frontin'. Help me to make you the priority of my life.
—Amen

"**A**ll the single ladies, now put your hands... DOWN!" Down? Yes, down. I don't care what Beyonce says. Don't seek to be seen. Wait to be won. You'll never see a fish sticking its head out of the water shouting, "Yoo-hoo! Oh Mr. Fisherman. Over here!" Desperation is not a good look, Ladies. Stop flagging men down. Let them seek you out.

CHEW ON THIS:

Then he went down and talked with the woman, and she was right in Samson's eyes. **[Judges 14:7]**

God,
Patience is the one fruit of
the spirit that's the hardest to
develop a taste for. Thank you
for being patient with me while
I work on it.
—Amen

H as "the bread of idleness" made you fat and lazy? Do you have the spiritual form of "I-tis?" Perhaps it's time to quit carb loading on the word and load up your car instead. Get in it and go get busy. Put the word into action! Don't know exactly what to do? Find someone who needs your help and use your gifts to improve their life. There's always plenty of work to be done. GET MOVIN' YOU LAZY LIMA BEAN!

CHEW ON THIS:

But do not forget to do good and to share, for with such sacrifices God is well pleased.
[Hebrews 13:16]

God,
Ok! I'm up! I'm up! I'm up!
—Amen

Unity is a destination that can only be reached when traveling as a group. Here are a few tips for a pleasant journey:
• Avoid complaining.
• Share your provisions.
• Look out for your fellow travelers.
• Don't be too proud to ask for directions.
• Stay with the tour!
Most importantly, don't panic if you get separated from the group. Your tour guide is the best at finding the lost. His name is Jesus.

CHEW ON THIS:

Behold, how good and how pleasant it is
For brethren to dwell together in unity!
[Psalm 133:1]

God,
I ask you to forgive me for the times I've rocked the boat and almost caused us all to drown.
I pray that I become a help and not a hindrance to my local assembly.
—Amen

W

ant more answers to your prayers? Then...SHUTTY!

Put your mouth on mute. Set your soul on silent and let God get a word in edgewise. Allow His voice to come through the noise of your problem. You might be surprised by what He has to say if you'd just LISTEN.

CHEW ON THIS:
Let all that I am wait quietly before God, for my hope is in Him. [**Psalm 62:5**]

God,
(ah...ah...ah...SHUTTY)
—Amen

If God were to give a SAT test, would you be able to pass it? Here's a sample question. Let's see how you do:

What is God's algebraic expression for the cause and effect of disobedience?

(Answer: If you do X don't ask Y Z happened.)

CHEW ON THIS:

Do not be deceived, God is not mocked; for whatever a man sows, that he will also reap. For he who sows to his flesh will of the flesh reap corruption, but he who sows to the Spirit will of the Spirit reap everlasting life. [**Galatians 6:7-8**]

God,
I've taken your kindness for weakness for too long. Please forgive me.
If there are consequences in play because of my disobedience, then I ask you to have mercy and give me the strength to endure them.
—Amen

You possess a gift that is uniquely yours. No one can do what you do quite the way you do it. But a gift serves no one if it is left in the box, tied tightly with a bow and shoved in a corner somewhere. Open up your gift and share it with the world. There are lives waiting to be changed by what's inside... including yours.

CHEW ON THIS:

As each one has received a gift, minister it to one another, as good stewards of the manifold grace of God. [1 Peter 4:10]

God,
I'm grateful for the life assignment you've given me. I will no longer take it for granted.
—Amen

Single Ladies, be careful that you don't devote more time to securing that diamond than you do to becoming "more precious than rubies." Your highest desire should not be the rock, but "the Rock." Be virtuous, not a vulture.

CHEW ON THIS:

Who can find a virtuous wife? For her worth is far above rubies. [**Proverbs 31:10**]

God,
I thank you that my marital status does not dictate my value, but the status of our relationship does.
—Amen

The late Ed Cole, founder of the Men's Christian Network, once said, "Above the clouds, the sun always shines." Today dark storm clouds may be gathering over your life, but please remember that clouds are always in motion. They blow in and out again. So brace yourself and prepare to ride it out. As I've always told my children, "The storm won't last forever." And I promise you, my angels, the sun will break through again for you. God cares about you and so do I.

CHEW ON THIS:

Fear not, for I am with you; Be not dismayed, for I am your God. I will strengthen you, Yes, I will help you, I will uphold you with My righteous right hand.' [Isaiah 41:10]

God,
You are the light that shines even on my darkest days. I am not afraid.
—Amen

W e've all done it. We've all had that DUH moment. Usually it's right after we've destroyed the entire house looking for our car keys, only to find them in the most obvious place. Well, if you've destroyed your life searching for the key to its true meaning, look no further. A life surrendered to Jesus Christ is where you'll find it. It is the most obvious place. DUH!

CHEW ON THIS:

For whoever desires to save his life will lose it, but whoever loses his life for My sake will find it. [**Matthew 16:25**]

Okay Jesus,
I give up. I've tried everything
else. If you're real, I need to know
you—today. I surrender all.
—Amen

Don't be a punk! It takes real courage to love people in this un-lovely world we live in. It means forgiving folks and letting stuff go. It means being vulnerable, taking a chance on being hurt and risking rejection. Do it anyway! Jesus did. Imagine where you'd be if He hadn't. So stop being a wuss. Man up!

CHEW ON THIS:

Beloved, if God so loved us, we also ought to love one another. [**1 John 4:11**]

God,
Cover me! I'm going in!
—Amen

D on't let that big number on your social media page fool you. It takes more than a click of a button to qualify as a friend.

CHEW ON THIS:

A man who has friends must show himself to be friendly. But there is a friend who sticks closer than a brother.
[Proverbs 18:24]

God,

Help me be a better friend to those I call "friend." Show me ways to look to their needs instead of dwelling on how they can meet mine.

—Amen

Have your words been a little bitter or sour lately? You may need to add some seasoned salt to bring out the flavor.

CHEW ON THIS:

Let your speech always be with grace, seasoned with salt, that you may know how you ought to answer each one.
[Colossians 4:6]

God,
I realize I've left a bad taste in the mouths of my friends and family by the way I talk to them. I've got some apologizing to do. Starting with you. I'm sorry.
—Amen

Celebrity news is all the rage, but does it really bring anything "Extra" into your life? Listen if you want "Access" to real good news, try a little less "TMZ" and a little more NIV. You just might find that the life of Peter is far more fascinating than the life of Bieber.

CHEW ON THIS:

For whatever things were written before were written for our learning, that we through the patience and comfort of the Scriptures might have hope. [**Romans 15:4**]

God,
Help me develop an obsession
for the "Good News."
—Amen

Babble says, "To be successful you must be the captain of your own destiny."

Bible says, "Many are the plans in the mind of a man, but it is the purpose of the Lord that will stand."

CHEW ON THIS:

There are many plans in a man's heart, Nevertheless the Lord's counsel—that will stand. **[Proverbs 19:21]**

God,
You are the creator of the universe. You know my comings and goings before I even think of them. So I gladly trade my plan for yours. Show me the way.
—Amen

[47]

God does not play hide and seek with us. He's not a game player. He's a game changer. Need direction for your life? Just ask Him for it. He'll gladly tell you. He wants you to live olly-olly-oxen-FREE!

CHEW ON THIS:

If any of you lacks wisdom, let him ask of God, who gives to all liberally and without reproach, and it will be given to him.
[James 1:5]

God,

I'm so tired of trying to figure it all out on my own. Please give me the wisdom I need to make the right decisions concerning my life. Thank you for your faithfulness. I truly appreciate it.

—Amen

The government may be able to outlaw a lot of things, but they can't legislate "light." So don't you dare dull your shine for nobody! Stand tall and show the world what you workin' with—Love, Joy, Peace, Patience, Kindness, Goodness, Faithfulness, Gentleness Self-Control. There ain't no law against these things. So no matter where you are—on the job, at school or wherever—go ahead and get your shine on!

CHEW ON THIS:

Let your light so shine before men, that they may see your good works and glorify your Father in heaven. [**Matthew 5:16**]

God,
I pray for the restoration of our government to a body that honors your law above the law of the land.
—Amen

Beware of picking roses from other people's gardens. They might be beautiful, but their thorns can be deadly. In other words: If he'll/she'll cheat WITH you, he'll/she'll cheat ON you.

CHEW ON THIS:

He who is faithful in what is least is faithful also in much; and he who is unjust in what is least is unjust also in much.
[Luke 16:10]

God,

Whether deceived or out of sheer rebellion, I have settled for less than your best for my life. But I don't want it anymore. I release him/her and return my heart to its rightful owner—You.

—Amen

Did you know that Atlanta-based rapper, Ludacris, sampled God?

It's true.

God was the first to spit: "When I move, you move. Just like that." Only when God said it, it sounded like this:

"I will instruct you and teach you in the way you should go; I will counsel you with my eye upon you." (Psalm 32:8)

If you're not sure which direction to go in life, pray. Then wait on the Lord. And when He moves you move—Just like that!

CHEW ON THIS:

In all your ways acknowledge Him, and He shall direct your paths. [**Proverbs 3:6**]

God,

I've got my eye on you.
Just say the word!

—Amen

[51]

The other day I complained to God about not having a steady income (as we freelance writers are sometimes wont to do). "How long will I have to live hand-to-mouth?" I whined. His response: *"Always. You will always have to live from my hand to your mouth."*

May we always remember to look to God for "our daily bread."

(Thanks for the reminder, Pastor Alex Pineda!)

CHEW ON THIS:
Give us this day our daily bread.
[Matthew 6:11]

God,
Thank you for supplying physical bread and bread from heaven. Both are so tasty!
—Amen

There is no nebulous grey area between good and evil. If it's not God, it's not good.

CHEW ON THIS:

Every good gift and every perfect gift is from above, and comes down from the Father of lights, with whom there is no variation or shadow of turning.
[James 1:17]

God,
Sharpen my discernment so that I will always know the difference.
—Amen

"Sic vox non vobis" is Latin for "Lay up, but not for ourselves." God never intended for you to hoard your talents. Somebody is in desperate need of what you do just naturally. Now, you may think, "Oh it's just a small thing." But little becomes much when placed in God's hands. So take your gifts out of lay-away! Quit laying it up and LAY IT OUT!!

CHEW ON THIS:

Having then gifts differing according to the grace that is given to us, let us use them: *if prophecy,* let us prophesy *in proportion to our faith.* [**1 Peter 4:10**]

God,
Remind me to be on the lookout for those divine opportunities to share the good news of your saving grace.
—Amen

Thinking about your problems too much? Get out of your own head and get into His.

CHEW ON THIS:

"So are My ways higher than your ways, And My thoughts than your thoughts."
[Isaiah 55:9]

God,
Please show me your ways.
Mine don't work.
—Amen

Your private relationship with God will be reflected in your public relationship with others.

CHEW ON THIS:

This is my commandment, that you love one another as I have loved you. **[John 15:12]**

God,
I know I've asked you to help me love others as you love them. But this time I really mean it.
—Amen

Would you ever tell God to his face that He made a mistake? Well, that's what we do every time we put ourselves down. Truth is, we are not qualified to critique God's creation. We'll get it wrong every time.

CHEW ON THIS:
I will praise You, for I am fearfully and wonderfully made; Marvelous are Your works, And that my soul knows very well.
[Psalm 139:14]

God,
Sorry. My bad.
—Amen

God is not blind. When Adam and Eve hid themselves in the garden, God asked where they were not because He couldn't find them, but because He wanted them to answer. He needed a confession. God sees and knows everything we do. Confessing our wrongdoing to Him sets the stage for the gracious act of forgiveness. So stop beating yourself up and 'fess up!

CHEW ON THIS:

If we confess our sin, He is faithful and just to forgive us our and to cleanse us from all unrighteousness. [**1 John 1:9**]

God,

I'm tired of trying to hide in plain sight. I confess I've fallen short of your glory. But I receive your forgiveness fully and I will not bring that mess up again. Thank you for loving me back into right standing with you. Onward.

—Amen

If you ever get an invitation from the Pity family, toss it. Don't even bother to RSVP. Trust me, the only person who would show up is you. Haven't you heard? Nobody likes a "Pity Party."

CHEW ON THIS:

Now may the God of hope fill you with all joy and peace in believing, that you may abound in hope by the power of the Holy Spirit. [**Romans 15:13**]

God,
With you it's always a
party of four—me, you,
Jesus and the Holy Spirit!
—Amen

Sometimes a brief and simple statement plainly spoken is more impacting than a litany of $5 words. While visiting my sister in Georgia recently, I heard one of the most dynamic quotes to ever come out of the pulpit on the subject of evangelism:

> 'You can't get it and put it in your pocket.
> We've got an obligation to share it.
> You might have your feelings on your shoulders and get rejected. But we've got to share it. How can they hear if they ain't never heard?'
> —REVEREND JAMES WRIGHT JR.,
> Emanuel Fellowship Church of Kennesaw, Georgia

Well said, Reverend Wright. Well said, indeed.

CHEW ON THIS:

And when you pray, do not use vain repetitions as the heathen do. For they think that they will be heard for their many words. [Matthew 6:7]

God,

Let me always shoot straight from the hip when sharing with others the message of your saving grace.

—Amen

I f grass looks greener on the other side it's only because it's covered in manure. If you're tempted to cheat on your spouse, remember this: The other woman/man may look good on the outside, but your relationship will be covered in waste and stink to the high heavens. Stay in your own yard. Water your own grass.

CHEW ON THIS:

Marriage is honorable among all, and the bed undefiled; but fornicators and adulterers God will judge. [**Hebrews 13:4**]

God,
You ain't got to tell me twice!
—Amen

Every farmer knows that he can't plow a straight line while looking at what's behind him. The same goes for us. We'll never move ahead with the call on our lives if we train our eyes on yesterday's failures.

If God had intended for us to walk in our past He would have screwed our feet on backwards. Keep moving forward. Your success is just ahead of you.

CHEW ON THIS:

"Do not remember the former things, Nor consider the things of old. Behold, I will do a new thing..." [Isaiah 43:18]

God,
You're gonna have to guide
my footsteps because
I'm fixing my eyes on you.
—Amen

The Greek lexicon defines the word "presence" as "face." So, if you want to know the path to life, and live a life filled with gladness, get all up in God's face. Because…

Love is in His face!

CHEW ON THIS:

No one has seen God at any time. If we love one another, God abides in us, and His love has been perfected in us. [**1 John 4:12**]

God,
I love being in your presence.
We should do this more often.
Same time tomorrow?
—Amen

When it comes to advice, be careful what you feed your soul. It's a ravenous creature that ain't got the sense God gave a turnip, and it will wolf down whatever nonsense and foolishness that tastes good. So eat the meat and spit out the bones of whatever you hear—even if it's from me.

CHEW ON THIS:

For the wisdom of this world is foolishness with God. For it is written, "He catches the wise in their own craftiness." **[1 Corinthians 3:19]**

God,
There are a lot of false teachers out there. Please give me the ability to sniff out the fakers.
—Amen

've heard it said that anything that drives you to your knees and into the presence of God is a good thing. Drive means "to propel or carry along by force in a specified direction." But wouldn't it be better if we didn't wait until stuff hits the fan before we hit our knees? Rather than being swept into His courts by the force of our circumstances, wouldn't God be more blessed by us coming into His presence voluntarily, with no agenda beyond being with Him? If anything is to drive us into His presence, let it be the desire to hear His heart in order to learn what fully pleases Him. Let's bless Him for a change.

CHEW ON THIS:

Bless the Lord, O my soul; And all that is within me, bless His holy name!
[Psalm 103:1]

God,
I don't want something to have to drive me to my knees. Let the promise of your presence be enough to compel me to come.
—Amen

N ever mind your mother. Would you kiss "The Father" with that mouth? Come on family, let's curb the swears. Profanity is not a good look on anybody—especially not on God's kids.

CHEW ON THIS:

Let no corrupt word proceed out of your mouth, but what is good for necessary edification, that it may impart grace to the hearers. [Ephesians 4:29]

God,
Uh oh! Be right back.
Gotta go gargle.
—Amen

A re you your husband's companion or his contractor? Well then put down that hammer and quit trying to renovate him! Remember: God is the master builder. Only He can weigh a heart and turn it wherever He wants. Try focusing on your own "Extreme Home Make-over" and "move that bus" in your own life instead of the one in his.

CHEW ON THIS:

The king's heart is in the hand of the Lord, Like the rivers of water; He turns it wherever He wishes. Every way of a man is right in his own eyes, But the Lord weighs the heart. **[Proverbs 21:1-2]**

God,

My husband is a development site that only you have the blueprints for. So I'm retiring from my construction job— effective immediately.

—Amen

Perhaps the reason you haven't found your Prince Charming is because you haven't been seeking the King of Kings. I'm just sayin'…

CHEW ON THIS:
You shall have no other Gods before me.
[Exodus 20:3]

God,
I apologize for trying to
rent out your throne.
—Amen

COMBO PLATES

Let the word of Christ dwell in you richly in all

wisdom, teaching and admonishing one another

in psalms and hymns and spiritual songs,

singing with grace in your hearts to the Lord.

[Colossians 3:16]

Let's Get It Crackin'

As she aged, my mother had to have all of her teeth extracted. We soon learned that Mama had the strongest gums of any human being God ever created. With her bare gums she could crack open a chicken bone, after which she would proceed to suck out the marrow (uh yeah...ewww). According to Mama, that's where the real nutrition was to be found—where the blood once ran.

When it comes to feeding on the Word of God, I've discovered that Mama had the right idea. In order to get to the real nutrition of the Bible we've got to clamp down on it until it cracks wide open—to where "the blood" runs. A quick glance at a passage while we have our morning coffee may satisfy the taste buds momentarily, but it's not until we take the time to crack open each word in search of its deepest meaning that we can enjoy its sustenance and transformative benefits. Sort of gives a whole new meaning to the term "Let's get it crackin'" doesn't it?

CHEW ON THIS:

"...making your ear attentive to wisdom and inclining your heart to understanding; yes, if you call out for insight and raise your voice for understanding, if you seek it like silver and search for it as for hidden treasures, then you will understand the fear of the Lord and find the knowledge of God." **[Proverbs 2:2-5]**

YOUR TO-GO ORDER

Pick one verse and spend this week cracking it open. Use a Bible dictionary, commentaries and/or lexicons to help you gain greater insight.

I Think You'd Better Call the Throne

One of the greatest privileges I have as a minister is the opportunity to pray with folks who are going through thangs. (Yes I said, "thangs.") Often people will reach out via e-mail, text or even by that old-fashioned method called, the telephone. But no matter how they contact me, their tone is telling. They are in need.

I find that many times it not about me offering them advice, but rather offering them an ear and a shoulder. However, when I'm asked to pray I never decline. But I am very clear. Yes, I believe God hears me. And yes, God does answer my prayers. But my words are not magic beans that will take you up to the giant God in the sky. Your faith has to take you into His presence.

God doesn't play favorites. He can (and will) answer your prayers as well as anybody's. So maybe next time before you run to phone a friend, dial up the throne room of God. Cut out the middleman and talk to Him directly. There are no toll charges and His line is always open.

CHEW ON THIS:

Hear me when I call, O God my righteousness! You have relieved me in my distress; Have mercy on me, and hear my prayer. **[Psalm 4:1]**

YOUR TO-GO ORDER

Ask yourself: How often do I rely on others to pray for me instead of praying for myself?

Got To or Get To?

Mama used to say that there are few things in life you absolutely have to do. I think her exact words were, "I ain't got to do nothin' but be Black and die." (Taking orders wasn't Mama's strong suit.)

I thought about Mama the other day as I listened to someone from our fellowship complain about having to wake up for the 5am prayer call. They used the words "got to" as in "I got to get up early tomorrow to pray." The thinly veiled irritation in their voice gave the impression that rising early to talk to God was more than a little inconvenience; it is an imposition, an obligatory task that they dreaded. WOW!

Now from where I sit the ability to rise in the morning and to converse with the Creator of the Universe is not a chore or a duty—it's a privilege. It's not a "got to," it's a "get to." We "get to" stand in the presence of the Almighty himself. We get to pour out our complaints at his feet with full confidence that he will address each and every one of them. We get to learn of his will and his ways in order to become more like him. We get to feel the warmth of his love as He lavishes it upon us. What a blessing to know that while we don't "got to" start our day with God, we "get to."

CHEW ON THIS:

Enter into His gates with thanksgiving, and into His courts with praise. Be thankful to Him, and bless His name. For the Lord is good; His mercy is everlasting, And His truth endures to all generations.
[Psalm 100:4-5]

YOUR TO-GO ORDER

Next time you're tempted to complain about something ask yourself—Is it a "got to" or a "get to."

The Velvet Rope of Heaven

Oh what a night I had last night! I was privileged to walk the red carpet at the World Premiere of the latest Disney masterpiece, "Saving Mr. Banks." Strolling beneath the bright lights past dozens upon dozens of reporters and camera crews from around the world, I felt as if I was starring in my own fairy tale.

I stood only a few feet away from some of Hollywood's giants and my personal favorites — Tom Hanks, Emma Thompson, as well as the incomparable Julie Andrews and Dick Van Dyke! It was major and for a moment I thought it just doesn't get any better than this.

Or does it?

There is a day coming when we who believe will walk heaven's red carpet. We shall stroll along the streets of gold and everywhere we look giants of the faith will surround us. Look over there! There's Paul! There's John, Moses and Abraham! How cool is that?

Then the moment will come when the trumpet shall sound and we will stand not before the gods

of men, but before the one true and living God—
The King of Kings and the Lord of Lords. When
we all get to heaven, oh what a day of rejoicing
that will be! You're invited. Won't you please
come? I promise it will be a blast!

CHEW ON THIS:

Jesus answered and said to him, "Most assuredly, I say to you, unless one is born again, he cannot see the kingdom of God." **[John 3:3]**

YOUR TO-GO ORDER

Reach out to God and tell him that you'd like to RSVP for Heaven's party. If you're reading this, I'm sure it's not too late to get on the list.

Monday, Monday

I overheard a conversation the other day in which someone whined about it being "Monday again." It made me stop and think about how we've come to assign different emotions to certain days. We groan about Manic Mondays, cheer about "Hump Day" (better known as Wednesday), and sing about "Living for the weekend 'cuz that's when we party down." But shouldn't we approach each day with equal excitement? I mean think about it. Isn't everyday above ground a cause to celebrate?

More importantly, with each new dawn comes new opportunities, new adventures, new mercies. I think that's something worth getting jazzed about. Sure some days will bring situations and circumstances that suck. Still, being alive one more day to live out the purpose of God is a pretty good deal. So instead of rising with a sense of dread, let's arise each and every day enthusiastically with these words in our hearts and on our lips—"This IS the day that the Lord has made. I WILL rejoice and be glad it in."

CHEW ON THIS:

This was the Lord's doing. It is marvelous in our eyes. **[Psalm 118:23]**

YOUR TO-GO ORDER

Tomorrow morning before you get out of bed just take a moment to say "Thank you."

It's All about Timing

Imagine that you're a brand new driver, in a brand new car, and you're making your first attempt ever to get onto the freeway. Your palms are sweaty. There are impatient drivers behind you. Hundreds of cars careen by at high speeds, some driven by people consuming everything from weed to Whoopers with cheese while behind the wheel. You remember what the driver's manual said about how to get into the flow of traffic. It said that you must watch for the light to turn green, yield to oncoming cars, and wait for the perfect time to merge. But what do you do? You decide to follow the example of others you've ahead of you. So you push the pedal to the metal and bogart your way into traffic!

Why, then, are you all freaked out because your car was hit? You're the one who got anxious and decided to do it your way. You decided not to follow the instructions in the manual. Well now, how's that working for you?

Listen my angel, God is not cruel. It's not his intention to torture us by asking us to wait patiently for answers to our prayers (even though it feels like it). There are a myriad of reasons why

God delays his answers. To keep us out of harm's way while we wait he says, "Be still." Don't move! Don't try and bogart your way into that relationship, that move, that career change, that nose job. Just wait until God gives you the green light. Only then can you merge safely in the flow of transition. Wherever God is taking you in life. Wait for his signal!

CHEW ON THIS:

For the vision is yet for an appointed time; But at the end it will speak, and it will not lie. Though it tarries, wait for it; Because it will surely come, It will not tarry.
[Habakkuk 2:3]

YOUR TO-GO ORDER

Feeling anxious about a decision you need to make? Pump your brakes and devote some time to praise. Praise God for the answer and the patience to wait for it.

[82]

Success Is a Battlefield

I admit it. I'm hooked on the game app, Word Battle. I play it when my brain needs a break from work. With this app, you and your opponents are given the same set of letters and are challenged to see who can make the highest scoring word in the best time.

When I first started playing Word Battle, I sucked. No, I really sucked. However, over time I gained experience and climbed the leaderboard. Also, I learned some valuable lessons on how to be successful not just in the game, but in the game of life. And I'd like to share them with you.

LIFE LESSONS LEARNED FROM PLAYING "WORD BATTLE" ON FACEBOOK

- Understand the rules before playing
- Be gracious to your opponents
- Put your best profile pic (face) forward
- Identify and utilize all available resources and tools
- Take risks, even if it makes you look foolish
- Be strategic
- Be aware of your opponents moves, but don't focus on them
- Learn from your mistakes; learn from theirs
- Don't wait too long to make a move
- Play against yourself; strive to beat your best

- Play with those with more experience. They'll make you better
- Don't get cocky; nobody like trash talkers
- Don't get greedy
- Pay attention; distractions can cost you the game
- Don't dump out early because you're down, you can comeback
- There's more than one way to do anything
- Congratulate others when they win
- Eliminated? Stick around and cheer somebody else on
- Play to win
- Give it a rest sometime
- Enjoy yourself
- Don't give up

CHEW ON THIS:

But he said, "What is impossible with men is possible with God." **[Luke 18:27]**

YOUR TO-GO ORDER

Remember, you've got the greatest coach ever in Christ.

So get out there and PLAY!

Are You in Good Hands?

Living in the Land of Luxury Cars (aka "Los Angeles"), it's easy to see how some can become self-conscious about the type of car they drive. Personally, I don't give a rip. When asked what I drive, I've been known to proudly answer, a 2005 "Paidfor." Despite the missing hubcap and noisy motor mount, I have no problem rolling my ride up to any valet parking stand in town as if it's a fresh-off-the-factory-line Bentley. They may look at me like I'm crazy, but I don't care. It's PAID FOR!

You see, it occurred to me one day that God doesn't care about what I drive either. He's more concerned about how I walk. So let me ask you: Is your walk brand new? Is it fully loaded with love? Is it registered in the Book of Life? How much prayer mileage do you get? Do your relationships have that new life smell?

Start this week by reviewing your existing "assurance" policy. Is it serving your current spiritual needs? If you find that you need to make a change, may I recommend the Lord's "Met Life?" He'll meet you right where you are? And with Him, you're in good hands because, like a good neighbor, the Lord is there. Jesus Christ is on your side. He guarantees that if you walk in the light of his love you'll always walk in style.

CHEW ON THIS:

Therefore be followers of God as dear children. And walk in love, as Christ also has loved us and given Himself for us, an offering and a sacrifice to God for a sweet-smelling aroma. **[Ephesians 5:1-2]**

YOUR TO-GO ORDER

Unlike taking a physical walk, there is no time to stop and rest when you're walking in love. Keep going!

Are You Sure?

Are you a child of God? Are you sure?

Before you answer, please read this:

"But to all who did receive him, who believed in his name, he gave the right to become children of God." (John 1:12)

AND THIS:

"For you are all sons of God through faith in Christ Jesus." (Galatians 3:26)

In light of these passages, can you say with assurance that you are a child of God?

If the answer is no, but you'd like to know for sure, please pray with me...

Jesus, I believe you are who the Bible says that you are. I believe you came down from heaven on a mission of love to save my soul; that the death you suffered on the cross was intended for me. Thank you for taking my place. I surrender all that I am and all that I have to you. You are now the Lord of my life. From now and throughout eternity you will reign and rule over all that concerns me. Thank you Jesus for giving me the right, at last, to be called a child of God. —Amen

If you prayed to receive Jesus Christ for the first time, welcome to the family! Or if you've just returned to the Lord, welcome home! Either way, would you let me know? I'd love to rejoice with you! Please drop me at line at www.morningmannathebook.com.

Horace

I heard him before I saw him. As I walked into the diner, I was greeted by the sound of an irritated, African American man, 60-ish, who sported a Kangol hat fashionably worn to the back, and who was raising all kinds of sand. He bombarded his companion with a litany of epithets that would have embarrassed Richard Pryor. But there was a sort of pained desperation in his plea:

"Stop putting things in my mind that don't belong there, Horace! &%$%* things in my mind that don't belong there make me weak, Horace! Don't do it. Please Horace!"

Now Horace, along with two waitresses, a random customer, and the restaurant manager tried in vain to get the man to lower his voice. The man was apologetic but still insisted that "Horace" was attempting to fill his mind with information that he was convinced would do him harm.

This went on for about 15 minutes before both men left the diner. I couldn't stop thinking about this man. It was clear that his mental state was questionable. Still, there was much truth in what he said.

Our thoughts have the power to make us weak.

Negative thoughts cause us to dwell on worse case scenarios that may never occur. Those thoughts can become even more real to us than reality and they can rob us precious mental, emotional, and spiritual energy. Speak to the "Horace" in your head. Tell him to stop putting things in your mind that don't belong there. Then replace those thoughts that tear you down with ones that lift you up.

CHEW ON THIS:

Finally, brethren, whatever things are true, whatever things are noble, whatever things are just, whatever things are pure, whatever things are lovely, whatever things are of good report, if there is any virtue and if there is anything praiseworthy—meditate on these things. [**Philippians 4:8**]

YOUR TO-GO ORDER

Search the scriptures for a promise or principle that debunks your negative thoughts. Make that your new thought.

Janky Joints

Osteoarthritis is a pain! (Pun intended). I've got OA in both knees. After an active weekend the pain runs a close second only to childbirth. Much of the damage could have been prevented had I shed a few pounds and gotten some exercise to strengthen the knee's supportive muscles. Shoulda, coulda, woulda. So now my bones clack together like a pair of chopsticks. I'm not as graceful on the dance floor as I once was, and even the way I walk is compromised. Truth is, I fall down...a lot.

The Biblical definition of the word "walk" is: live, conduct your life. How we walk out our spiritual lives is much like caring for our physical knees. If we carry around the excess weight of sins such as envy, lust, fear, worry, pride, or unforgiveness, our walk will be compromised. If we fail to "exercise" by studying the scriptures and participating in fellowship with other believers our lives become weakened and we will fall down...a lot.

This week, let's purpose in our hearts walk strongly before the Lord. Let's shed the weight and strengthen our knees. Only then we can truly walk worthy of the calling with which we were called.

CHEW ON THIS:

Therefore strengthen the hands which hang down, and the feeble knees, and make straight paths for your feet, so that what is lame may not be dislocated, but rather be healed. **[Hebrews 12:12-13]**

YOUR TO-GO ORDER

Carrying extra weight is a killer on the knees. Next time you pray imagine that your concerns are heavy packages. See yourself handing them off to Christ. You'll feel lighter, I promise.

Private Eyes

Did you know that God wrote the very first stalker song? Long before Sting sang, "Every breath you take...I'll be watching you," long before Aretha sang, "I'm gonna rap on your door, tap on your window pane..," and even before Bobby Brown sang, "Every little step you take...," God said:

"I will never leave you nor forsake you. I'll be with you always."

Although the evening news would have you believe otherwise, God's presence can be felt by those who seek Him—even in the midst of mayhem. The week ahead may present you with many challenges, but be of good courage! God is omnipresent. He's everywhere—all the time. He is never further than a prayer away.

What joy it is to realize that even if you feel lonely at times you're never truly alone. If your life is fully surrendered to God you can confidently sing along with R&B one-hit wonder, Rockwell:

"I always feel like somebody's watching me."

CHEW ON THIS:

And the Lord, he is the one who goes before you. He will be with you. He will not leave you nor forsake you; do not fear nor be dismayed. **[Deuteronomy 31:8]**

YOUR TO-GO ORDER

Can you think of a time when you were sure God was present? What were you doing? How did it make you feel?

A Handful of Gimme

Okay, admit it. We all know someone we hate to see coming because they always show up with a handful of gimme. If it's not "Let me hold a coupla dollahs," it's "Can you watch Starnisha and Ray-Ray while I run to Target?" It's rare that these individuals reach out to us just to say "Wassup?" or "How you doin'?"

But isn't that how we approach God? Instead of coming to Him just to spend time in His presence, we show up in prayer with a laundry list of things we want Him to do.

It's not that God hates to see us coming. He loves us. In fact, Luke 12:32 tells us that it is the Father's good pleasure to give us the kingdom. He delights in answering our prayers. But He also wants us to develop the desire to just "be" in His presence simply because we love Him. He wants us to approach Him not with a handful of gimme, but rather with empty hands that He can fill with the things that can only be found in His presence.

CHEW ON THIS:

You will show me the path of life; In Your presence is fullness of joy; At Your right hand are pleasures forevermore.
[Psalm 16:11]

YOUR TO-GO ORDER

Today, go to God for His presence, not just His presents.

Yes, He Will (I Think)

Just thinking of my Mama and remembering how sometimes I'd overhear her singing during her morning devotion. Often she'd sing, "I know the Lord will make a way. Oh yes He will." Perhaps you've sung that song yourself, hoping that the Lord would make a way out of a situation you found yourself in. But let me ask you this: **Will the Lord really make a way for you?**

Yeah I said it. Wait! Before you get all scrunchy-faced, take a closer look at what the song says: **"I know the Lord..."**

Ah ha! And herein lies the trouble for a lot of people. They don't "know" he will because they don't know Him. They can merely hope he will answer their prayers. Having true faith in God is contingent on having a relationship with him. Where there is no relationship, prayers may be going unanswered.

A casual glance at the Bible every once-in-a-while, desperate 11th hour prayers when stuff hits the fan, and periodic Sunday morning trips to the church house do not a relationship make. Go to God with the intent to really get to know him.

Know for yourself that he can and will make a way. "Oh yes He will!"

CHEW ON THIS:

For this reason we also, since the day we heard it, do not cease to pray for you, and to ask that you may be filled with the knowledge of His will in all wisdom and spiritual understanding; that you may have a walk worthy of the Lord, fully pleasing Him, being fruitful in every good work and increasing in the knowledge of God.
[Colossians 1: 9-10]

YOUR TO-GO ORDER

If someone were to ask you to show them proof that you know Jesus Christ, what would you show them?

It's Not a Game

Let me ask you "The $64,000 Question"—Have you made a "Love Connection" with God? If not, please don't "Press Your Luck." "To Tell the Truth," avoiding Him will only get you a whammy from Satan. I kid you not, "The Joker's Wild." He's the enemy of your soul. He'll try and entice you by saying, "So You Want to Be a Millionaire?" Okay, "Let's Make a Deal." But don't spin his "Wheel of Fortune" because it'll only put you in "Jeopardy" of being lost for eternity.

It's time to choose "Truth or Consequences." Show the devil that you "Are Smarter Than a 5th Grader." Go ahead. "Beat the Clock" and surrender your life to Jesus Christ today. He is the "Password" to your salvation and the ultimate "Big Brother." Take the "American Bible Challenge" and learn of Him. Let His love transform you into a "Survivor." Listen, I'm not trying to start a "Family Feud." I promise you that this is no "$10,000 Pyramid" scheme. It is truly a "Match Game" made in heaven. And "The Price is Right"—Eternal life with God is free to all who believe. So what do you say? "Deal or No Deal?"

CHEW ON THIS:

Most assuredly, I say to you, he who hears My word and believes in Him who sent Me has everlasting life, and shall not come into judgment, but has passed from death into life. **[John 5:24]**

YOUR TO-GO ORDER

What sort of games are you still trying to run on God?

Nothin' For Something

Back in the day, R&B legend Billy Preston had a hit called, "Nothin' From Nothin.'" It went, in part, "Nothin' from nothin' leaves nothin'. You gotta have somethin' if you wanna be with me." But God says— You gotta have NOTHIN' if you wanna be with me.

A life of true intimacy with God means we have to empty ourselves. We have to empty our soul of its selfish ambitions and self-pleasing passions. When we're empty of our self-centered agendas we can step into His presence unhindered. And it's then, and only then, that He can fill our empty places with desires and dreams of *His* design.

CHEW ON THIS:
I have suffered the loss of all things, and count them as rubbish, that I may gain Christ. [**Philippians 3:8b**]

YOUR TO-GO ORDER

Next time you pray go to God empty because in His economy you'll always receive something for nothin'.

Use Your Words

Today I did a face plant on the mat of life. My soul was down for the count. Battered and bruised by temptation, I raised the white towel high in the air and was just about to throw it in when I heard the Holy Spirit say..."Use your words."

Well, duh! Why hadn't I thought of that? Use my words.

In the heat of the moment I'd forgotten the first line of defense against temptation: Use the words that God has given me. In the midst of a temptation is the time to recall his instructions and promises. When we regularly ingest scripture it helps us to build a resistance to temptation. His word becomes our defense. It is the most effective weapon we have when the enemy body attempts to body slam us.

Envision Jesus in the wilderness, his stomach hollow and rumbling from 40 days of starvation, his lips cracked and bleeding from a lack of water. Satan came and offered him a way out. Throw in the towel and I'll give you what your soul desires—relief. But Jesus was not to be enticed to defeat. Instead, the Savior used his words—"And Jesus answering said unto him, It is said, Thou shalt not tempt the Lord thy God." (Luke 4:12) That was it. Game. Set. Match. Satan was forced to leave the building.

If you find yourself in a wrestling match with temptation, use your words—the word of the Lord that resides in you—and knock that joker smooth out!

CHEW ON THIS:
Thy word have I hid in mine heart, that I might not sin against thee. [**Psalm 119:11**]

YOUR TO-GO ORDER

Get in the habit of speaking scripture out loud. Faith comes by hearing.

Country Parables

People who think I'm funny obviously have never met some of my kinfolk. My "baby brother" Shelby Stokes is a country boy to the bone. Everything about him says crawdads and coon huntin.' And his deep Southness is the deepest when he's preaching the gospel. Those of us who know and love him call his unique way of sharing the word, "Country Parables." You haven't lived until you've heard him preach one of his patented country classics such as "That Dog Don't Hunt" and most recently, "Stay Sof" (not "soft," but "sof").

According to Brother Shelby, "In order for us be used by God we must keep ourselves in a position of submissive, obedient, faith." In other words, we've got to stay SOF. What a fitting word for a world whose moral arteries are hardening faster than a Pappy's snuff can in a blizzard. A world where people outside and inside Christianity are moving away from God and toward a sort of self-sufficient spirituality; A world where it's hip to be a Hell-raiser and rebellion is worn as a badge of honor. Where submission and obedience have become dirty words.

So please keep sharing your country parables Bro. Shelby Stokes. You're serving up some tasty, life-sustaining vittles, my angel. God bless all of the front line soldiers bringing the gospel to the masses on street corners around the world everyday of the week.

CHEW ON THIS:

"Bless is the one who reverences the Lord always, but whoever hardens his heart will fall into calamity." [**Proverbs 28:14**]

YOUR TO-GO ORDER

Think of at least one thing you can do this week to support an evangelistic street ministry in your area.

You so Crazy

It's time to stop trippin' about this life. Jesus Christ came so we can live fully in peace and with joy in the here and now—not just in eternity. So why are you trippin' about jobs and cars and people and other temporal things? I'll tell you why— YOU'RE CRAZY!

Allowing the spirit of fear to go unchecked will make you crazy. I know. I was crazy for a long time. Fear trapped me and made me weak, mean, and crazy. Fear will cause you to think, say, and do things so far out of character that you'll even scare yourself. Don't believe me? Ask your family how crazy you look when you're stressed out.

The good news is that there's help that doesn't require a straight-jacket and copious amounts of mood-enhancing drugs. It's called, Prayer. The next time you trip over the tests and trials of life, go ahead and fall to your knees. You might just find power, love, and your sound mind while you're down there.

CHEW ON THIS:
For God hath not given us the spirit of fear; but of power, and of love, and of a sound mind. [2 Timothy 1:7]

YOUR TO-GO ORDER

For just a moment, allow yourself to think of the worst case scenario should that thing you fear actually happen. Now is it still bigger than God?

Sink or Swim

Call me a stereotype, if you will. A coward, if you must. But I am a Black person who cannot swim. From where I sit, submersing myself in water equals suffocation, equals death, equals people showing up at my family's house wearing black and carrying Bundt cakes. Not an exciting prospect. So I avoid pools, hot tubs, oceans, and such.

It's not like I haven't tried though. Once I even took a water safety class. Within moments of the first session, I began to sink. I was drowning! As my lungs quickly filled with water, I heard a voice in my muffled ears. The voice said, "T. Faye! Stand up." It was my instructor. I was only in three feet of water.

Fear will do that to you. Your situation looks overwhelming and you're convinced that you're going to drown. So you thrash around desperately (making quite a spectacle of yourself). But God is faithful. He will never let you down or let you drown. He's a very present help in a time of trouble. He is our strength and a refuge. (Psalm 46:1)

If you're facing rising waters in your job, in your marriage, with your children or friends, reach out for God. He is the ultimate lifeguard.

CHEW ON THIS:

He sent from above, He took me; He drew me out of many waters. He delivered me from my strong enemy, From those who hated me, For they were too strong for me. They confronted me in the day of calamity. But the Lord was my support.
[Psalm 18:16-19]

YOUR TO-GO ORDER

STAND UP! In Jesus' name!

A Cup of Love

Once upon a time, when women still wore their drawers underneath their clothes and men got jobs and moved out of their mama's house before the age of 40, people actually knew their neighbors. If somebody needed to make Kool-Aid and ran out of sugar, they could grab a cup, pop next door to 3B and borrow some.

Not so today. We've evolved into a cloistered culture where we live behind steel doors, safely peering out at the world from our personal space and never inviting anyone in. We move quickly from our cars to our front doors, eyes to the ground so as to avoid contact with people who live only yards away.

So the question is:

How can we love our neighbor if we don't know our neighbor?

Answer: We can't. And if we can't love our neighbor, how can we fulfill the greatest of all commandments? — "Love the Lord your God with all your heart and with all your soul and with all your mind and with all your strength...Love your neighbor as yourself." (Mark 12:29-31) There's only one way. Go to God with the empty cup called your heart and let Him fill it with kindness, patience, humility, and goodness.

CHEW ON THIS:
Let all that you do be done with love.
[1 Corinthians 16:14]

YOUR TO-GO ORDER

Pop over to 3B and share a cup of love with your neighbor. (Yes, even that one.)

Be a Charlie

In the children's classic, "Charlie and the Chocolate Factory," candy maker Willy Wonka sets out to find the child who would someday run his fabled mill. Likewise, God is looking for someone to run his factory. He is looking for heirs to His kingdom. But before you raise your hand and say, "Ooo! Ooo! God pick me!" ask yourself: How am I like the children in the story? Am I a manipulative brat like Veruca Salt, treating the Father like a cash cow? Throwing tantrums when God doesn't give me my way? Or am I a glutton like Augustus Gloop? Living to satisfy the lust of my flesh only to discover that nothing truly satisfies? Do I live to be entertained like Mike TV? Preferring to plug into the world instead of the Word? Knowing more about Maroon 5 than Matthew 5? Or am I an annoying know-it-all, bloated with pride like Violet Beauregard? Insisting on doing things my way?

To become true heirs of the kingdom, our goal should be Charlie Bucket. Yes, Charlie fell into temptation when he stole Fizzy Lifting Drinks. But Charlie also confessed and repented of his sin. It is when we confess our sins, turn from our wicked ways and totally surrender our Everlasting Gob Stoppers back to God that he not only forgives us, but he gives us the keys to his kingdom. Sweet!

CHEW ON THIS:

The Spirit Himself bears witness with our spirit that we are children of God, and if children, then heirs—heirs of God and joint heirs with Christ, if indeed we suffer with Him, that we may also be glorified together.
[Romans 8:16-17]

YOUR TO-GO ORDER

Identify the character flaws that are preventing you from being a "Charlie."

Why Are You Making It Complicated?

Perhaps you've seen those annoying commercials extolling the virtues of a well-known vocational college. You know the ones with the attitudinal, but very cute Black dude in the baseball cap who urges people to "get off the couch" and enroll in classes? Yeah, that one. Well today, I'm that guy!

You know what God has told you to do. You heard his still small voice giving you clear direction. And you know it wasn't your idea because most likely what you heard is something that will take you out of your comfort-zone or require you to let go of something (or someone) you've been hanging onto for dear life.

You also know what God has told you not to do. Even if you've haven't heard his voice about what not to do, you have 66 books of instruction to use as a point of reference. There are no excuses.

So, what are you waiting for? Why are you still sitting there in disobedience?

Let me make this easy for you: You know what God said to do. So do it! You know what God said not to do. So don't do it. It doesn't get anymore clear than that! As the dude in the commercial says, "Why are you making it complicated? It's easy."

CHEW ON THIS:
Why do you call me 'Lord, Lord' and not do what I tell you? **[Luke 6:46]**

YOUR TO-GO ORDER

Get on your knees right now! Call God and ask his forgiveness for your disobedience and get started on your future today. Do it now!

What's the Song in Your Heart?

This morning, while "In The Garden" alone, I entered into a "Sweet Hour of Prayer." I said to the Lord, "Here I Am to Worship" and immediately His "Love Lifted Me." I began to reflect back on when I first found myself "At the Cross." It was there that I discovered "There is a Fountain Filled with Blood," and "The Blood" cleansed me and made me brand new. It was there that I began "Leaning on the Everlasting Arms." I discovered "What a Friend We Have in Jesus" and realized that He is, indeed, my "Rock of Ages." And "As the Deer" that pants for water to quench its thirst, so I longed to be with Him. It was there that my heart cried, "Draw Me Nearer" "Precious Lord."

Call me crazy for believing as I do. But "I Know My Redeemer Lives." Call me fanatical if I "Go Tell It on the Mountain." But I know firsthand "How Great is Our God." And although "I'm a Soldier (In the Army of the Lord)," I would be nothing if not for His "Amazing Grace." If you don't know this Savior I speak of, please trust and believe me when I say "Because He Lives" you can face tomorrow. You can have the "Blessed Assurance" of an abundant and eternal life. "There is a Balm in Gilead" that will heal your hurts and give you hope. "Softly and Tenderly" Jesus is calling your name. Please answer: "Have Thine Own Way, Lord," "Take My Life and Let It Be Consecrated Unto Thee." I promise you'll find that "'Tis So Sweet to Trust in Jesus."

CHEW ON THIS:

Oh, sing to the Lord a new song! Sing to the Lord, all the earth. [Psalm 96:1]

YOUR TO-GO ORDER

Sing the song in your heart.

Via Veritas Vita

You may have finished the "Twelve Step Program," mastered all "7 Habits of Highly Effective People," agreed with "The Four Agreements," (You might even be down with the "Fifty Shades of Grey." I ain't judgin' you, Boo-Boo). But if you truly desire to reach the place of complete freedom, peace, and satisfaction, there is only ONE WAY and it is simply this: "Jesus said, I am the way, the truth and the life. No man can come to the Father except through me."

So come to Jesus today, my angel. Hand over to Him all of the cares and concerns, the tragedies and yes, even the triumphs of your life. It's easy. Simply believe that Jesus Christ is who he says he is. Open your mouth and tell him that you believe it. Then place your life into his very capable hands. This one decision will change your life forever.

CHEW ON THIS:

Jesus said to him, "I am the way, the truth, and the life. No one comes to the Father except through Me. [John 14:6]

YOUR TO-GO ORDER

BELIEVE. CONFESS. LIVE!

Let's Talk About Love...Lost

On the list of inevitable life events, lost love ranks pretty high—somewhere after death and taxes. Whether it's a crushing break-up with a high school sweetheart or a devastating divorce, if you're breathing you will experience the sting of lost love at least once in your lifetime.

But is what we call "love" really love?

One of my favorite songs is the Al Green hit, "Let's Stay Together." It speaks of weathering the storms of love; of holding on "whether times are good or bad or happy or sad." If 1 Corinthians is to be believed, then it is apparently possible to stay even when everything in you says, "Go."

True love chooses to trust. True love has hope in even in the most hopeless of situations. True love is tenacious. It doesn't just walk away because it got too hard. That is not the character of true love.

So why can't we seem to follow Brother Al's advice? Could it be that the thing we call "love" isn't really love?

With the above definition in mind, think about

your own love relationships—romantic or otherwise and ask yourself:

- Do I trust my loved one? Can I be trusted?
- Am I in this relationship for the duration?
- What are my hopes for this relationship?

Remember: Even good relationships can get gooder.

CHEW ON THIS:

"[Love]...always protects. It always trusts. It always hopes. It never gives up."
[1 Corinthians 13:7]

YOUR TO-GO ORDER

Ask yourself: Is it love, lust or loneliness?

Daddy Clean

My mother was a domestic. Growing up I spent my summers and school holidays working side-by-side with her emptying ashtrays, pumice stoning toilets, and changing linens in some of the ritziest homes in Southern California.

Mama's exacting standards was evident in our own home as well, and as a result to this day I don't consider my apartment to be truly clean until it is "Mama clean." Mama clean is scrub-with-a-toothbrush-in-the-corners-behind-stuff-that-nobody-but-you-will-ever-see-clean. It's hard work.

Perhaps that is why I'm so grateful that my life is "Daddy clean." It takes no work at all. I simply asked my Heavenly Father to forgive me of all my sin, to cleanse me from all unrighteousness and just like that it's done.

Now don't get it twisted, God has exacting standards, too. Once He's done the work He fully expects us to keep the house clean. Yes, He is faithful and will always forgive us when we fall short. But that does not give us a pass to keep junkin' up the place on purpose. Instead we are to "Make every effort to live in peace with everyone and to be holy; without holiness no one will see the Lord."

CHEW ON THIS:
For God did not call us to uncleanness, but in holiness. **[1 Thessalonians 4:7]**

YOUR TO-GO ORDER

Pretend for a moment a child asks you what it means to be holy. How would you explain it?

Then, He Walked In

Many moons ago when my sons were young, they played in the same Pee-Wee basketball league as the son of Academy Award-winning actor, Denzel Washington. I'll always remember the day my boy's team first played J.D.'s team.

It was about 15 minutes or so into the first quarter, when suddenly the atmosphere in the gymnasium shifted. I kid you not, I felt him before I saw him. I turned to look over my shoulder just as the doors opened, and with his trademark ultra-cool stride, in walks one of yummiest of all of God's creations.

I cannot tell you the final score of that game, but I can tell you that everything about that day changed the moment Denzel Washington entered the building.

My point this morning is this: While we cannot see the Holy Spirit, we can certainly feel him. His presence becomes more than apparent when he enters because the very moment we invite him into our lives everything about it changes. Suddenly we have divine direction, uncommon peace, unexplainable joy, and boundless love. We experience new levels of faith, gentleness, longsuffering, goodness and self-control.

By the way, Denzel and his wife, Pauletta treated both teams to KFC after the game. Now the Holy Spirit may not buy you fried chicken, but he will always provide you with comfort food.

CHEW ON THIS:

But you shall receive power when the Holy Spirit has come upon you; and you shall be witnesses to Me in Jerusalem, and in all Judea and Samaria, and to the end of the earth. **[Acts 1:8]**

YOUR TO-GO ORDER

Question: Are you certain that the Holy Spirit has come upon you? What makes you so sure? Not sure? Re-read Acts 1.

Suit Up!

Life is a battle. Flaming arrows of fear, frustration, and disappointment are lobbed at you every day. But too many times you've found yourself in the middle of the battlefield, bucket-naked with just a helmet on and the enemy's darts hangin' out your backside while you stand there singing, "Jesus be a fence all around me."

Look, just getting saved is not all there is to this fight. Satan is a crafty so-and-so. Therefore, we must put on the full armor to resist his tactics. First, we need to strap truth around waist. Our life should be one of sincerity. The breastplate of righteousness guards our hearts and enables us to make right choices. The battlefield is littered with landmines, so we're to wear the gospel of peace on our feet to protect us from the explosions of temptation. And most importantly, the shield of faith must be carried at all times.

Note that the armor offers no back protection. Why? Because we are to advance on the enemy, never retreat.

So remember: Before going into battle— SUIT UP!

CHEW ON THIS:

"Therefore take up the whole armor of God, that you may be able to withstand in the evil day." **[Ephesians 6:13a]**

YOUR TO-GO ORDER

Check your armor. Are there any missing or rusty pieces? What will you do today to become battle ready?

Butterflies in the Belly

As I prepared to walk out on stage at a recent speaking engagement, I asked the pastor if he had any sage words of wisdom to share about his congregation. With a knowing twinkle in his eye, he simply said, "God is for you." It struck me that he either sensed the presence of the butterflies flitting about in my belly or that he was just trying to say, "Brace yourself. They are going to eat you alive."

Whatever the reason, his words stuck with me—God is for you. I thought about those four simple words for many days afterward—God is for you. I thought of Romans 8:31 "What then shall we say to these things? If God is for us, who can be against us?" I thought—God is not just WITH us. He is FOR us. God is on our side. God's got our best interest at heart. He's cheering us on.

God wants us to win.

It is the very nature of God to want to see his children excel. He's committed to our success, and he's spared no expense to ensure that we do. The life of Christ was the price God paid so that we can walk victoriously and joyfully in in our marriages, with our children, on our jobs, and among our friends.

So even with butterflies in your belly, step out onto the stage of your life knowing this—"God is for you."

CHEW ON THIS:

Have I not commanded you? Be strong and of good courage; do not be afraid, nor be dismayed, for the Lord your God is with you wherever you go. **[Joshua 1:9]**

YOUR TO-GO ORDER

God wants you to win but you've got to believe it. Do you?

Take Him Down

"No that little booger didn't work his way into my office!" was all I could think as I watched a wayward wasp squeeze his body through a gap in the window screen. I had spied him circling the window, but because there was a screen (and the window was only slightly cracked) I figured there was no danger. Not only did that sucker get in the room, he proceeded to create total chaos. Picture me trying to take him down with an organic, non-harmful bug spray. Yeah, right. He sipped that through a straw like Kool-Aid. Then he came after me. I was expelled from my own office by a creature smaller than my pinky toe. A quick trip to the hardware store and I returned armed with some heavy artillery. He was no match for the can with a skull and cross bones on the label. Death came quickly. (So did the stains on my curtains and carpet. But I digress.) The enemy was gone. I won!

What has this got to do with anything, you ask? Well, simply this—The devil is a wasp! He works his way into the smallest of openings in your soul—a gossiping tongue, a funky attitude, an ungodly relationship. Next thing you know, he's infiltrated your life and chased you away from what is rightfully yours—the peace and blessings of God. You can't be mamby-pambying around with some lightweight, fruity-scented positive thinking, self-help nonsense. You've got to pull out the big guns and take that joker down. The unadulterated word of the living God in your heart and on your lips is what takes down the devil. "It is written!"

CHEW ON THIS:

For the word of God is living and powerful, and sharper than any two-edged sword, piercing even to the division of soul and spirit, and of joints and marrow, and is a discerner of the thoughts and intents of the heart. **[Hebrews 4:12]**

YOUR TO-GO ORDER

Identify an area of your life where the enemy has worked his way in. Now commit to memory a Biblical principle with which you can combat him and knock the snot out of him!

[130]

Running On Empty

Car manufacturers say that driving a car when the gas meter is hovering around "E" puts a strain on the engine because old sediment in the tank begins to circulate. As a result the car starts to run sluggishly.

Even if a car is a bucket, it will run more efficiently when the gas tank is full. We can apply that to our walk with the Lord. If we don't keep our lives topped off with the Word, we'll get sluggish and our walk will become a crawl. Soon we'll just stall out all together.

The best plan is fill up every day. Even if you meditate on just a scripture or two every day, your life will begin to run more efficiently.

CHEW ON THIS:
This Book of the Law shall not depart from your mouth, but you shall meditate in it day and night, that you may observe to do according to all that is written in it. For then you will make your way prosperous, and then you will have good success. **[Joshua 1:8]**

YOUR TO-GO ORDER

Fill 'er up!

Lost In "No Way"

Picture this: There you are traveling along in life, and even though the road is clearly marked with signposts to guide you, you decide to ignore them and go your own way. Too proud or too ashamed to ask for directions, you make several wrong turns. Before long darkness falls, you become disoriented and panicky. There seems to be no way out of the situation you've gotten yourself into! You're lost in the Land of Noway.

Sound familiar?

Trust me. I know of which I speak. Recently I got lost. I made a decision to go my own way, do my own thing, blow past the signposts of guidance that God clearly placed along the road of my life. The result? I wound up lost in Noway. But thanks be to God who always leads us to triumph in Christ! He made a way out of "no way." He patiently led me out of Noway into a broad place of liberty and restoration. My God is the ultimate GPS.

Today if you find yourself in Noway driving around in circles just frustrated and frightened, go to the road map—the Bible, get to the callbox—prayer, listen to the traffic reporter—the Holy Spirit.

Get God's coordinates for your life and allow Him
to make for you a way out of Noway.

CHEW ON THIS:

*"In all your ways acknowledge him, and he will
make straight your paths."* [**Proverbs 3:6**]

YOUR TO-GO ORDER

What or who in your life is blocking the signposts God has put up for you? What steps do you need to take to clear your view?

Eat Before You Come

The very funny comedienne Roz Browne tells a great story about her wedding and how she saved money by telling her guests to eat before coming to the reception. Hilarious! Can you imagine being invited to an event known for free food only to be told there would be none? Would you still go?

How many times have you heard someone say that they left a particular church or fellowship because they weren't "getting fed"? Perhaps you've said it once or twice yourself (I know I have). But here's the real—If your Bible is sitting in the same spot you left it when you came home from church last Sunday, its no wonder you're "hungry."

Now before you get all scrunchy-faced, I know there are some churches that tend to serve lighter fare, and that can be frustrating if you desire a meal that's more substantial. But if you know that pastor serves only PB&J, don't get all bent out of shape because you want steak. First of all, that pastor is not solely responsible for making sure you get full. Secondly, you're the one who rolled up to that particular church in the first place. Are you sure God sent you there? Uh-huh...

Listen, if the Lord sent you there and you feel like you're not "getting fed" then you'd better pack a snack and stay put until He releases you to go elsewhere. You just may have an assignment there.

You see, just like attending a wedding, church isn't really about you. It's about worshipping God by serving the person seated next to you. It's about preparing ourselves to reach out beyond the church walls to a lost and dying world which needs an encounter with the Almighty. It's about God's kids coming together to grow together, to support one another, learning from each other and most importantly, loving one another. Though important, it's NOT about a 30-45 minute message designed to fill you up for the next six days.

CHEW ON THIS:

Till I come, give attention to reading, to exhortation, to doctrine. **[1 Timothy 4:13]**

YOUR TO-GO ORDER

Still feeling a bit peckish after service? Grab some people and head over to the nearest diner. Discuss the message. There's nothing more satisfying than food and conversation—especially if the Word is on the menu.

Angel in an Apron

Mama Ella died. And if you live in or have visited the metropolitan area of Los Angeles chances are you've encountered this iconic woman. For 28 years she served plates piled high with chicken and waffles at the landmark eatery that started the international craze, Roscoe's House of Chicken and Waffles. Her homespun, but no-nonsense demeanor charmed thousands and even inspired a loving spoof on sketch comedy series, "In Living Color."

To Mama Ella, people were people. From gangbangers to church ladies to potentates to A-list celebrities, she served them all with equal efficiency and care, and didn't think twice about telling any one of them to take their elbows off the table if the occasion called for it. She was a server in the highest order. Proud of her vocation and diligent in her work, she elevated waitressing to a craft.

So the next time you sit down in a restaurant, pay attention to the person serving you. It just might be an angel in an apron.

Mama Ella, it's your turn to take a seat at the

banquet table and be served. God bless and rest you. You taught us well and you will be missed.

CHEW ON THIS:

Do not forget to entertain strangers, for by so doing some have unwittingly entertained angels. **[Hebrews 13:2]**

YOUR TO-GO ORDER

Make a mental list of the people you bypass on a daily basis. Prayerfully consider which of them you can reach out to and get to know.

Are You a Pro?

If you're like me you tend to put the "pro" in "procrastination." Why is it that we perpetually prolong carrying out God's plan when He's spoken so clearly to us about His expectations for our careers, finances, relationships, ministries?

I'll tell you why.

It's because procrastination is a by-product of perfectionism, and perfectionism, not to be confused with the desire to do things well, is produced by pride. We don't move because we're afraid we'll get it wrong. And good-googly-moogly, God forbid we make a mistake! After all, what will people say? When us "pros" think we can't do it perfectly we don't do it all. That's pride, and pride always precedes a fall (Proverbs 16:18). Ouch!

But here's some motivation for change: There's a lot of work to be done for the kingdom. People are lost and dying because we're afraid to try. It's time for us to step out into the imperfect and allow God to perfect it. It's a little thing He likes to call, "faith." So now, this day, I declare and decree that I will no longer be a "pro."

But I will get the job done!

CHEW ON THIS:

See then that you walk circumspectly, not as fools but as wise, redeeming the time, because the days are evil.
[Ephesians 5:15-16]

YOUR TO-GO ORDER

What will you do today to be less "perfect?"

Bark Like a Dog

In the modern classic film "Coming to America," there's an iconic scene in which Prince Hakeem (played to the hilt by Eddie Murphy) meets the woman chosen by his parents to be his wife. Trained since birth to serve the prince, Princess Imani (the delightful Vanessa Bell Calloway) refuses to disobey any of the prince's commands. She even obeys when he orders her to hop on one foot and bark like a dog—"arf arf arf...WOOF WOOF WOOF." It's hilarious!

Although it's played for yucks, the scene is a great object lesson for us. Her desire to be fully pleasing to her master at all costs is exactly how we should live for God. We should be so committed to obeying Him that we don't care how crazy it makes us look.

Now I'm not suggesting that the Lord will ever ask us to do anything as humiliating as barking like a dog, but He does require us to do wacky things like love our enemies and be kind to those who despitefully use us. He asks us to be calm in the midst of the worst storms of our lives. And though He knows we can't swim, He commands us to step out of the boat and to walk on water with Him. And our response should always be "Yes my Lord. Whatever you like."

CHEW ON THIS:

But Peter and the other apostles answered and said: "We ought to obey God rather than men. **[Colossians 1:9-10]**

YOUR TO-GO ORDER

Say "yes" to the Lord.

Don't question it. Just do it!

#TBT

In social media Thursdays are designated as, "Throwback Thursday." It's a day of fun in which people post old school photographs of themselves and friends online with the hashtag #TBT. Some of the pictures are downright hilarious. There we are, in all our glory, sporting Kid 'n Play high-top fades, Billy Ray Cyrus mullets, Madonna lace and Hammer pants. At that time you could not tell us that we were not fly. Looking back at the good times is great fun. But, if I may, I'd like to propose that Throwback Thursday also serve as a reminder to "throw Thursday back."

Isn't it time we throw back the bad memories of Thursdays past? Why not let #TBT be the day you throw back the unforgiveness you've carried for those who did you wrong way back when. Throw back the guilt and shame you feel because of that thing you did that no one knows about. Throw back the regrets over broken promises and missed opportunities.

God stands ready to give our lives a brand new, fresh-to-def look when we surrender our yesterdays to Him. In fact, you don't even have to wait until Thursday. Make today the day you throw back the pain of the past and allow Him to post new hashtags on our lives. #Forgiven #Redeemed #Renewed #Revived #Setfree

CHEW ON THIS:

For I know the plans I have for you," declares the LORD, "plans to prosper you and not to harm you, plans to give you hope and a future. **[Jeremiah 29:11]**

YOUR TO-GO ORDER

Let them go. Move on. It's time.

HEART HEALTHY MENU

Keep your heart with all diligence,

For out of it **spring** *the issues of life.*

[Proverbs 4:23]

Te Amo

One of my favorite movies of all-time is "Moonstruck." There's a great scene in which the father has been caught creepin'. In his frustration and guilt he says to his wife, "A man discovers that his life has been for nothing and that's a bad crazy day." Although she's been betrayed by the man she loves, she responds with much tenderness and strength— "Your life has not been for nothin'. Te Amo."

Te Amo—I love you.

If you feel that your life lacks purpose. If you can't see why you're even here on this planet. I want you to know that if nobody appreciates you, if nobody gets you, if you feel invisible, God is saying to you today: Your life has not been for nothin'. Te Amo.

Perhaps you've found yourself caught up in that same sin over and over again. Maybe you feel like there's no way God will forgive you for betraying him time and time again. Beloved, God is saying to you today: Your life has not been for nothin'. Te Amo.

You are loved beyond measure by the one who

invented love, my angel. You are never so far out of reach that his love cannot take hold of your heart. Please, please don't ever forget that.

CHEW ON THIS:
For God so loved the world that he gave his one and only Son, that whoever believes in him shall not perish but have eternal life. For God did not send his Son into the world to condemn the world, but to save the world through him.
[John 3:16-17]

"I believe that unarmed truth and unconditional love will have the final word in reality. This is why right, temporarily defeated, is stronger than evil triumphant."

—Reverend Martin Luther King, Jr.

Get Up! It's Morning.

This entry is being written during a very difficult time. There's no other way to say it other than simply—I'm going through some thangs y'all. But who isn't? Life happens. Things turn on a dime. Fortunes are made and lost. People love and leave. Health and wellness become sickness and dis-ease.

"Yet will I praise Him."

Whatever your season of transition looks like, please know that you are not forgotten. God does, indeed, know your name. And while you might feel as if you can't take one more day of the pain, of the uncertainty, of the lack or loss, here's one thing I know like I know my name—If you can wake up, you can still get up. So don't you dare let the current chaos crush your spirit, my angel. Keep dreaming. Keep hoping. Keep pushing. Keep believing. Keep it together. Keep your head up. Keep the faith. Don't you dare give up. GET UP!

CHEW ON THIS:

"For his anger lasts only a moment, but his favor lasts a lifetime; weeping may stay for the night, but rejoicing comes in the morning." **[Psalm 30:5]**

"When you get into a tight place and everything goes against you, till it seems as though you could not hang on a minute longer, never give up then, for that is just the place and time that the tide will turn."

—Harriet Beecher Stowe

Where Are You?

We've all done it. We've all worn God like an accessory we put on to beautify our lives only to take Him off when He no longer matches what we want to wear. But then, life happens...hard. And just like we scrabble to find the lost backing to our favorite pair of earrings, we scrabble in the darkest of our nights, in the depth of our despair to find God.

Our petitions are set in platinum promises. "Lord, if you get me through this I'll serve you all the..." "I will tell everybody about your goodness and..." "God I love you..."

Then, the sun shines again and His mercy is tucked away in the back of a drawer. Our prayers become shorter. Worship is relegated to one fast song and two slow on Sunday mornings...if we go. Our testimony becomes an anecdote we tell sometimes at parties. And we are good until... Life happens. Again.

"Oh God! Where are you?"

But the real question is? Where are YOU?

Where are you on the bright, carefree days when all is right in your world? When the bills are paid and the spouse is acting right? Are you still rising early or staying up late to be in His presence? Are you still digging for the precious gems of the promises of His word? Where are you?

CHEW ON THIS:

For although they knew God, they did not honor him as God or give thanks to him, but they became futile in their thinking, and their foolish hearts were darkened.
[Romans 1:21]

"Too many Christians have a commitment of convenience. They'll stay faithful as long as it's safe and doesn't involve risk, rejection, or criticism."

— Dr. Charles Stanley

Break a Leg!

In 2014, the babies of the baby boomers hit the Big 5-0, bringing millions one step closer to retirement age. With freshly minted AARP cards in hand, some envision days of leisure, new opportunities, and new adventures. But many approach this phase of life with trepidation. Regrets over a lack of retirement planning spark fear. You worry: "Will I survive financially?" "How long will I have to work?" "What will I do if my health goes South?" Okay, so now that you've totally freaked yourself out, here's the good news...

THE BEST PART OF THE SHOW USUALLY HAPPENS IN THE SECOND ACT.

This is your time to shine! Never before have seniors been more empowered to make decisions that can impact not only their future, but that of the world-at-large. Finally, our voices are being heard from the church house to the schoolhouse to the White House. But we have to believe that we are valuable before we expect anyone else to.

Listen, your life experience can influence generations to come if you'll only share it. Those gray hairs that you and Clariol keep trying to cover up are symbols of well-earned wisdom and a crown of knowledge—something that cannot be bought at any price.

There is so much more ahead for you to accomplish. So what if your knees are janky and you can't run. You can walk and talk with a youngster who's having trouble in school. So what if you can no longer see without your glasses. Put them on and read to someone who can't see at all.

Most importantly, we must never stop learning. Even us seniors could use a refresher course in Godly living. Paul wrote: Teach the older men to be temperate, worthy of respect, self-controlled, and sound in faith, in love and in endurance. Likewise, the older women to be reverent in the way they live, not to be slanderers or addicted to much wine, but to teach what is good." (Titus 2:1-3)

So retiring minds want to know: What does retirement really mean? It means it's time to retire your regrets over the things you always meant to do but didn't and get busy with what you can do! So places ere'body! The curtain is going up! Break a leg! (But please, not your hip!)

CHEW ON THIS:

Even to your old age, I am He, And even to gray hairs I will carry you! I have made, and will bear; Even I will carry and will deliver you. [**Isaiah 46:4**]

"Aging has a wonderful beauty and we should have respect for that."

—Eartha Kitt

What's It All About?

I woke up this morning with a song looping in my head. It was not a get-yo'-behind-outta-bed-and-get-it-in-gear praise song. Nor was it a fall-on-you-face-before-the-Lord song of worship. But I woke up humming the theme song from the 1966 film, "Alfie."

"What's it all about, Alfie? Is just for the moment we live?"

I confess I didn't know all of the words, so I Googled it. (Don't you just love Google?) My eyes quickly fell upon one line that stood out from the rest:

"As sure as I believe there's a heaven above, Alfie; I know there's something much more. Something even non-believers can believe in; I believe in love, Alfie."

Yes! We all can believe in love. Even the most jaded of us. Those who have been hurt in love, those who have sworn off of it can still harbor a glimmer of hope that love is, indeed, a many splendored thing.

Love makes the world go 'round. Love takes time. Love is all you need—So many lyrics written to try and define love. But truth is, it only takes three words—GOD IS LOVE.

He is the embodiment, the personification of all that love is. And if we know Him, then we know what true love is.

I believe in love, Alfie. In fact, I know him intimately. Do you?

CHEW ON THIS:

Beloved, let us love one another, for love is of God; and everyone who loves is born of God and knows God. He who does not love does not know God, for God is love.
[1 John 4:7-8]

"God is love. He didn't need us. But he wanted us. And that is the most amazing thing."
—Rick Warren

Stop! Thief!

In my stand-up routine I sometimes tell this joke:

My great grandfather was sort of a black Robin Hood. If you came into the 'hood, he robbed you.

But the real thief in life is fear. Fear is a bandit so crafty that it will rob you of the power to reason and cause you to make irrational decisions. Fear is so insidious it will make you afraid of your own gifts. It will paralyze you. When that happens both you and those around you suffer loss. The quality of someone's life is compromised because you're afraid to move in your gifts. But here's the good news...

For God has not given us a spirit of fear, but of power, of love and of a sound mind. (2 Timothy 1:7)

Beloved, take it from a former fraidy cat, you don't have to be afraid to do, to go, to try, to dream, to hope, to plan. God has got your back. You can depend on Him to uphold you in the battle. And yes, you will encounter some on the way. But be of good courage, Christ came to make straight the path to victory and to stop the thief from stealing your joy!

CHEW ON THIS:
Whenever I'm afraid, I will trust in you.
[Psalm 56:3]

"We can easily forgive a child who is afraid of the dark; the real tragedy of life is when men are afraid of the light."

—Plato

Walk Past Your Past

Recently, I participated in a very intense personal growth seminar. During one of the exercises we were asked to think back to the most painful experience of our lives. The instruction was to visualize and recreate that moment in our minds, and to allow ourselves to "feel the pain as if it just happened."

I tried. Really I did.

But an awesome thing occurred when I attempted to conjure up those feelings of hurt and bitterness that used to plague me. I found that what had been the most painful experience no longer hurt. The pain that I once thought would kill me was no longer there. It had lost its power to paralyze me.

And God did it.

When God heals, he flings our hurts as far as the east is from the west. We no longer have to mull over the memories. There is no need to revisit the past. Why come out of your pocket for something that has already been paid for? Jesus paid the price for your pain. So why are you still trying to tip the devil?

The past is over and done. Walk in your freedom.

CHEW ON THIS:
Remember not the former things, nor consider the things of old. Behold, I am doing a new thing; now it springs forth, do you not perceive it? I will make a way in the wilderness and rivers in the desert.
[Isaiah 43:18-19]

"You can live your life angry, bitter, mad at somebody or even guilty, not letting go of your own mistakes, but you won't receive the good things God has in store."

—Joel Osteen

What's in Your Basket?

Now that the chill of winter is finally setting in, I find myself jones'n for the taste of the grape tomatoes that my friend Jan grew in her backyard this past summer. Patiently attended to with love and care, they were the sweetest tomatoes I've ever tasted. I'm talkin' a pop of sunshine in every bite. Luckily she experienced a bumper crop and shared them generously. It gave me just one more reason to look forward to seeing my green-thumbed friend. Not only would I receive enough tomatoes to fill a basket, I'd get one of Jan's patented warm smiles and even warmer hugs.

I pray that we experience our own bumper crop of fruit–the fruit of the Holy Spirit. (Yes, tomato is a fruit.) May we have bushels filled with love, joy, peace, patience, kindness, goodness, faithfulness, gentleness and self-control. So much so that people love to see us coming, and that everyone we come into contact with will walk away with a basketful of our tastiest fruit.

CHEW ON THIS:

But the fruit of the Spirit is love, joy, peace, patience, kindness, goodness, faithfulness, gentleness and self-control. Against such there is no law. [**Galatians 5:22-23**]

"Love is a fruit in season at all times, and within reach of every hand."
—Mother Teresa

Be-U-To-the-Full

Do you often feel alone in a crowd? Do you look around the room and make comparisons? Do you feel that everyone else is somehow more interesting, beautiful, clever, or funny than you are? Well, I've walked miles in your shoes and I'm here to tell you that…

YOU DON'T HAVE TO LIVE THIS WAY!

The criticism we heap upon ourselves, and the subsequent desire to measure up to some unrealistic ideal, begins early in childhood. The result? We grow into adults who waste a lifetime seeking acceptance and inclusion. Instead of living in the fullness of who we are naturally, we spend fortunes trying to alter our appearance. We exchange personal integrity for popularity. We reshape our perspectives just to fit in.

I implore you to embrace the individual God created you to be. He took great pains to give you unique qualities that cannot be duplicated by anyone. Your fingerprints are uniquely yours. Even the two halves of your body are completely different from one another. Love that about yourself. As my dear friend Comedian Bone Hampton so eloquently puts it, "Be comfortable with yo' self!"

Hide this truth in your heart today: **"I am fearfully and wonderfully made."**—Psalm 139:14

Then, as soon as you possibly can, I want you to take your unique self across that room and introduce it to another unique person. Enjoy learning about what makes them different and celebrate those differences.

And always remember, you have a custom-designed destiny. There is something God wants you to do that no one else can do quite the way you can. Someone is anxiously waiting to make your acquaintance (even though they don't know it yet). There is someone who needs what you have to offer. Their life will be incomplete until you suit up and show up in the fullness of who you are.

Please, just Be-U-to-the-Full!

CHEW ON THIS:
Then God said, Let us make man in Our image, according to Our likeness.
[Genesis 1:26]

"Always be yourself, express yourself, have faith in yourself."

—Bruce Lee

Happy

I defy anyone to resist cracking a smile while listening to Pharrell Williams' runaway hit song, "Happy." The tune just makes you feel...well... happy. It sort of reminds me of Bobby McFerrin's big hit, "Don't Worry Be Happy." The infectious little ditty, written for the soundtrack of the animated film "Despicable Me 2," earned the wunderkind singer-songwriter-producer an Academy Award nomination and has created smiles for millions of people around the world. The song says, in part:

"Clap along if you feel like a room without a roof. Clap along if you feel like happiness is the truth. Clap along if you know what happiness is to you."

The question on the kitchen table this morning is:

Do you know what happiness is to YOU?

The dictionary defines "happiness" as "a state of well-being and contentment." The Bible calls it being "blessed." So when you read passages that begin with "Blessed is the man..." translate it to "Happy is the man..." or "Content and in a state of well-being is the man..." Do that and I've got a feeling you just might find yourself smiling. Here, try it:

Happy is the man whose God is the Lord.
(Psalm 144:15)

Happy is the man who trusts in the Lord.
(Jeremiah 17:7)`

Happy is the man who finds wisdom.
(Proverbs 3:13)

Happy is the man who fears the Lord.
(Psalm 112:1)

Happy is the man whose sin the Lord will
not take into account.
(Romans 4:8)

Happy is the man whose rebellion is forgiven.
(Psalm 32:1)

Happy is the man who places his
confidence in the Lord.
(Psalm 40:4)

Now, if you're happy and you know it, clap your hands! See? Told ya! ☺

What Have You Done for Him Lately?

Driving past one of LA's many mega churches, I found myself projecting the cost of the towering sanctuary and lamenting what I deemed to be excess spending. It was a beautiful building to be sure, but my attention was drawn away from its stunning architecture to the sidewalk running along the front.

My eyes followed the parade of humanity that marched past the iron gates surrounding the building. I watched a constant stream of people moving from point A to B; people who represented every kind of disenfranchisement imaginable.

Suddenly, I was angry. Why doesn't someone come out from the behind those expensive stained glass windows, unchain the gates and attend to the needs of the people right under their noses? For shame, I thought.

Then it happened.

That still small voice dropped a question into my heart. "What have YOU done in the past 24 hours to meet the need of someone else?"

Ouch.

CHEW ON THIS (I know I will):
"Judge not, that you be not judged. For with what judgment you judge, you will be judged; and with the measure you use, it will be measured back to you. And why do you look at the speck in your brother's eye, but do not consider the plank in your own eye? **[Matthew 7:1-3]**

"What does love look like? It has the hands to help others. It has the feet to hasten to the poor and needy. It has eyes to see misery and want. It has the ears to hear the sighs and sorrows of men. That is what love looks like."
—St. Augustine

The Early Bird Gets the Manna

At this writing I am in Georgia. Not the bustling metropolis of Atlanta, mind you. Oh noooo. I'm visiting my sister who recently moved to Kennesaw, Georgia. We're talkin' the deeeeeeep South where Walmart is the hot spot and the sidewalks (where there are sidewalks) roll up at sundown. This place is so laid back that my sister's pastor cancelled mid-week bible study in order to go fishing for supplies for the fish fry on Saturday. True story.

This place is beyond quaint. The grass is, in fact, greener, the sun hotter, and the sky bluer than what I'm accustomed to back home in Los Angeles. It's absolutely beautiful. Opie, Andy, and Aunt Bee would have been very happy in Kennesaw.

I'll admit the slower pace has had an impact on me. This morning I sat and stared out of a window for the better part of an hour. I watched little creatures scurrying about the wooded area behind my sister's home. A lone bird caught my attention as he hopped around on the grass looking for insects to eat. Unfortunately for him, he had little success. Why? Because, he was late. Really late.

It was neigh on 10am. Where was he at 5:30 when all the other birds were doing their marketing? It was clear that he had missed out as the choicest bits had already snatched up. I sort of felt sorry for him. But you know what they about the early bird. And so it is with us.

In order to hear God with clarity, to receive the choicest bits of His guidance, we must seek Him early. David wrote, "Let me hear in the morning of your steadfast love, for in you I trust. Make me know the way I should go, for to you I lift up my soul." (Psalm 143:8)

Jesus often rose early while it was still dark to pray. It was in the still and solitude of the hours before dawn that he communed with the Father. There were no distractions, nothing to steal away his attention. He could worship God with laser focus and as a result, Jesus always heard God's voice with clarity.

Let us rise and seek the presence of God early in our day. Now understand I'm not getting legalistic on you. If you work nights and your "morning" doesn't begin until 1 o'clock in the afternoon. Cool.

Devote the first part of your "morning" in prayer and to the study of scripture. Because here's the real deal, the day is coming when seeking God won't be an option. So don't be late!

CHEW ON THIS:

Seek the Lord while He may be found, Call upon him while he is near.
[Isaiah 55:6]

"God instructed Abraham to be habitual in walking with Him and living for Him. We can do this by establishing daily habits of prayer, worship and regular, consistent time spent in His Word."

—Joyce Meyer

Keep Going!

On a recent flight out of Los Angeles International Airport (LAX), I noticed a huge signpost on the runway. Painted in caution light yellow and with large black lettering the sign read: DO NOT TURN BEFORE REACHING THE SHORELINE.

If you've ever travelled from LAX heading east you know that most planes are required to fly west out over the Pacific Ocean then make a U-turn to get on course. The sign serves as a reminder to the navigator that turning too soon is a dangerous maneuver. Taking a shortcut could lead to disaster.

Isn't our journey to living a holy life like that? We're often tempted to take a shortcut. Or worse, we decide to turn around and go back to our past. Fortunately, we're blessed to have the signpost of the Holy Spirit on the runway to keep us on course. He constantly reminds us not to turn too soon. If we follow his directions will reach our final destination safely.

CHEW ON THIS:

Brothers, I do not consider that I have made it my own. But one thing I do: forgetting what lies behind and straining forward to what lies ahead. [**Philippians 3:13**]

"Close the door on the past."
—Johnny Cash

My Imaginary Friend

Growing up I spent a lot of time playing alone with my imaginary friends. I'd spend hours creating stories for them and acting them out. But in time they disappeared along with other childhood artifacts (like my beloved Jackson 5 album collection, which I suspect was pilfered when I left home to enter the Army). But I digress.

The habit of talking to someone we can't see should never leave us just because we grow up. Though we cannot see God, we can (and should) still have conversations with Him—all the time. He is a loyal companion who is ever present. I feel the comfort of His presence even when I'm in crowded room. Inside jokes between us make me smile and I'm sure people wonder if I've lost my mind when I break out in a smile or sigh a contented "ahhh" for no apparent reason. His presence is so tangible that it encompasses me. He is my very real friend and the author of my imagination.

CHEW ON THIS:

The Lord is near to all who call upon Him, To all who call upon Him in truth.
[Psalm 135:18]

"God is a circle whose center is everywhere and circumference is nowhere."

—Timaeus of Locri, Philosopher

A Voice in the Crowd

On a recent visit to Dodger Stadium, I witnessed something extraordinary. It was the bottom of the 9th, the score tied with two men on. Up to bat was not a power hitter, but the team's pitcher. The crowd let loose a collective groan. It was clear. We were doomed to extra innings. Then, it happened...

Suddenly, from somewhere down at the other end of my row came a tiny, hope-filled voice that said, "You can do it." It belonged to a little girl who couldn't have been more than six. She spoke so softly I was amazed she could be heard over the din of 50,000+ people. Though her voice was barely audible, the faith in her words rang loudly. She believed.

And so it is with us when we are faced with difficulties. The still small voice of God whispers, "You can do it." If we can only hear him, we would believe too.

God continually speaks; offering clarity, direction, and comfort. But the responsibility of hearing him falls to us. Yet, you won't hear him if you don't know him. John 10:27 reads: "My sheep hear my voice, and I know them, and they follow me." Take time to cultivate a relationship with God. Study scripture. Pray. Know the heart of God. Once you come into the sweetness of His presence, you'll find that the clamor of the world's opinion will fade to a hush and His still small voice will rise above the crowd saying, "You can do it."

CHEW ON THIS:

I can do all things through Christ who strengthens me. [**Philippians 4:13**]

"You can do what you have to do, and sometimes you can do it even better than you think you can."

—Jimmy Carter

Where Is the Love?

If you've never experienced the sort of intimacy with God where it feels as if you can feel his breath on your face, I'm here to tell you that it's something that, in the moment, you never want to end. But sadly, if one is not careful, it does end. The concerns of life roll up on you and BOOM! Suddenly you'll feel far away from God as spending time alone with Him becomes a mere bullet point that tumbles further and further down the to-do list.

Recently, I found myself sensing a growing distance between me and God. I had to ask myself why. The answer was simple. I had become distracted by life. I had fallen back into old habits of allowing circumstances to circumvent my fellowship with Him and with other believers. While I was assured of his promise that nothing would separate me from the love he has for me, He still felt very far away. I could no longer feel his breath on my face. The moment of critical mass came when I heard these words in my spirit:

"You've made your first love last instead of making your first love last."

WOW! Are you bold enough to ask yourself: Is

my love for God in last place? Or, is it everlasting?
Where is the love?

CHEW ON THIS:
*Nevertheless, I have this against you,
that you have left your first love."*
[Revelation 2:4]

"Those who know God the best are the richest and most powerful in prayer. Little acquaintance with God, and strangeness and coldness to Him, make prayer a rare and feeble thing."

—EM Bounds

Ask the Beasts

Driving home one rainy evening, I found myself mesmerized by patterns formed by the drops of water on my windshield. As the wipers rhythmically swiped back and forth, an infinite number of designs were created.

The next day I paused to contemplate droplets that clung to the leaves of the ficus tree outside the picture window of my living room. Struck again by the beauty of the sight, suddenly I was brought to tears by the meticulous care God takes in creating beauty with something as simple as a raindrop. But I would have missed it had I not taken the time to stop and look.

Unfortunately, at this time in history, bling has replaced birds. We'd rather watch a PBS special about nature than actually go outside and see it for ourselves. God's handiwork is a marvel that we don't seem to value. And what we don't value we eventually lose.

Pity.

CHEW ON THIS:

But ask the beasts, and they will teach you; the birds of the heavens, and they will tell you; or the bushes of the earth, and they will teach you; and the fish of the sea will declare to you. Who among all these does not know that the hand of the Lord has done this? In his hand is the life of every living thing and the breath of all mankind." **[Job 12:7-10]**

"Everybody needs beauty as well as bread, places to play in and pray in, where nature may heal and give strength to body and soul."

—John Muir

Heavy Manna

This plate of manna was inspired by a comment made by one of the "diners" who reads the weekly Morning Manna blog. In response to a particularly intense post she simply wrote:

"HEAVY!!!...but the truth is seldom light."

She was absolutely right. The total truth of God's word is, as she said, heavy. Which is why we usually prefer the lighter fare of the word. We love to hear that we're "the head and not the tail, above and not beneath"; how "the blessings of the Lord maketh rich and He adds no sorrow to it" and how He will give us the desires of our hearts.

But what about the more hearty manna? They are promises, too, if not exactly light. Truths like: "The wages of sin is death but the free gift of God is eternal life in Christ Jesus" Or "I am the way, the truth and the life. No man comes to the Father except by me."

Listen to me family, an unbalanced diet of God's promises to bless and prosper will leave you with spiritual rickets. The soul will go unchanged and the spirit will be malnourished. We need His words of correction as well in order to grow strong in the

Lord and in the power of His might.

So I hope you'll spend some time chewing on some "heavy" truths from the word of God. I know I will. Bon appetit!

CHEW ON THIS:

And you shall know the truth, and the truth shall make you free. **[John 8:32]**

"God offers to every mind its choice between truth and repose. Take which you please—you can never have both."

—Ralph Waldo Emerson

Compassion Not Convenience

He was stationed outside the door of the Post Office, a filthy football jersey on his back and an even filthier Styrofoam cup in his hand. I felt as if I could smell him before I opened my car door. In an attempt to avoid his solicitation, I circled around the back of my car swinging wide from where he stood. Still, I wasn't far enough not to hear his request: "Some change Ma'am?" I muttered a curt "No" and hurried into the lobby to pick up a check that was waiting for me in my box.

I had barely turned the key when conviction fell on me like the Dallas Cowboys defensive line. I fished a few coins out of my purse and on the way out sheepishly dropped them into his cup. "God bless you Ma'am," he responded to the sound of the coins. It was then that I realized he was blind.

The chastening God exacted in my spirit was swift and painful. He quickly reminded me that, "Compassion will never be convenient or comfortable." In that moment I repented and asked Him for forgiveness. I also prayed that I would no longer be stingy or selfish with my possessions or my person; And to be reminded that my life is not my own. I AM MY BROTHER'S KEEPER. And like you, I too am growing in grace day-by-day I am so grateful that He loves us enough not to leave us as we are.

CHEW ON THIS:

I have shown you in every way, by laboring like this, that you must support the weak. And remember the words of the Lord Jesus, that He said, 'It is more blessed to give than to receive.'"
[Acts 20:35]

"Our human compassion binds us the one to the other—not in pity or patronizingly, but as human beings who have learnt how to turn our common suffering into hope for the future."

—Nelson Mandela

Believe and Trust

I love listening to Black folks talk. I do. We have a way of turning a phrase that is just as colorful as our skin. I particularly love it when someone buttons a statement by saying, "Oh trust and believe" to signify that they mean what they say in no uncertain terms.

Oh trust and believe, Honey!

I often think about how we miss out on receiving the fullness of God's promises, because we believe but don't trust. We believe that he said it. But we don't trust that he'll do it.

Will God really heal me? Did God really intend for me to have peace of mind during hard times? Can God really provide for me financially? Can God really save my entire family?

Why don't we trust that God's word applies to us? In a word: Because we don't really know Him.

My bestie Melodie would lay down her life for mine. When she gives me her word, it is bond. That is fact. I know it like I know my name. I know her character and so I trust her with my life. When you know someone's character you can rely on them to keep their word.

CHEW ON THIS:

Therefore know that the Lord your God, He is God, the faithful God who keeps covenant and mercy for a thousand generations with those who love Him and keep His commandments.
[Deuteronomy 7:9]

"Once you become aware that the main business that you are here for is to know God, most of life's problems fall into place of their own accord."

—J.I. Packer

Live At Eye Level

The Book of Daniel tells of the life of King Nebuchadnezzar. He was the power hungry, idol-worshipping, oppressive monarch who took the children of Israel captive and carried them into Babylon. If you've never read this account, you should. Game of Thrones ain't got nothing on the Old Testament.

Anyway, for ole King Neb it was all about power, possessions and preeminence. He trained his eyes on the things he could obtain here on earth. Influenced by what he could see, he ultimately paid a great price for his actions. He went stark raving, screamin' mee-mee mad.

He was driven away from people and ate grass like the ox. His body was drenched with the dew of heaven until his hair grew like the feathers of an eagle and his nails like the claws of a bird.

But something miraculous happened while he was out scratching around for grubs in the wildness. He looked up.

Later he would recount the story, "At the end of that time, I, Nebuchadnezzar, raised my eyes toward heaven, and my sanity was restored. Then

I praised the Most High; I honored and glorified him who lives forever."

And so here we are. Influenced by commercials and magazine ads; corner offices and parking spaces with our names on them. We are driven to have more, do more, be more and it's making us crazy! But like King Neb, it will only change when we humble ourselves and lift our eyes towards God. Only then will our sanity be restored.

CHEW ON THIS:
Humble thyself in the sight of the Lord and He will lift you up. **[James 4:10]**

"A man can counterfeit love, he can counterfeit faith, he can counterfeit hope and all the other graces, but it is very difficult to counterfeit humility.

—D.L. Moody

The Smooth Path

Walking along the jogging path at a local park, I noticed a great number of footprints in the sandy track. It reminded me of an old dance step chart from Arthur Murray that illustrates how to tango. Footprints were going in every direction. It occurred to me that if I tried to follow those footprints it would take forever to reach the end of the track.

Our lives are much like that. With so many paths from which to choose, it's easy to be confused about which direction to take. Too often we try and follow the well-worn path others have taken only to veer off in the wrong direction, go in circles or worse, not move at all.

But take some advice from the wisest man who ever lived, King Solomon. He prayed and asked God to, "Make straight the path for thy feet, and all thy ways shall be established." We are to level or smooth out the path we walk by removing any obstacles or distractions that could cause us to make false steps. Then our journey becomes secure and we can reach the end with certainty and in triumph.

CHEW ON THIS:
For you were once darkness, but now you are light in the Lord. Walk as children of light. [**Ephesians 5:8**]

"If you're walking down the right path and you're willing to keep walking, eventually you'll make progress."
—President Barack Obama

Smooth

Of all the people in the Bible, Nehemiah is my favorite (after the Father, the Son and the Holy Spirit, of course). I'm telling you, Nehemiah is my dude. Bold, courageous, and a visionary, he was just smooth with it. I think of when he supervised the rebuilding of the Jerusalem wall and a messenger came to warn him of an assassination plot. The man suggested that Nehemiah hide in the temple. But to the threat my man Nehemiah responded, "Should a man such as I flee?"

Nehemiah wasn't cocky, he was simply confident. Confident in knowing what he was called by God to accomplish.

We see this trait in the first chapter of his self-titled book. Nehemiah writes of how he went into his boss's office and asked for an extended leave to go build a wall. Not a strange request except Nehemiah was not a contractor. He was a cup bearer, and his boss was the king. No matter. He was confident that God had put it in his heart to return to his native city and help his brothers rebuild the Jerusalem wall. He was so impressive, the King gave him time off and all the resources he'd need to get the job done. Confidence. May we all develop such confidence in our callings so we, too, can be smooth with it in troubled times.

CHEW ON THIS:

In the fear of the Lord there is strong confidence, And His children will have a place of refuge. [**Proverbs 14:26**]

"I am not moved by what I see. I am not moved by what I feel. I am moved only by what I believe."

—Smith Wigglesworth

SIDE ORDERS

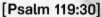

The entrance of Your words gives light;

It gives understanding to the simple.

[Psalm 119:30]

Your ~~Lucky~~ Blessed Day

You wanna hear God's Oprah impression? It goes something like this:

"This morning...YOU GET A NEW MERCY! YOU GET A NEW MERCY! YOU GET A NEW MERCY!"

Be encouraged today my angels. That thing you did that you're still feeling guilty about? Let it go! Repent, pray for forgiveness and keep it pushing. God is not trippin'. Remember that the steadfast love of the Lord NEVER ceases; His loving kindnesses NEVER come to an end. They are new each and EVERY morning for great is His faithfulness towards you. Grace and peace to you!

CHEW ON THIS:

Through the Lord's mercies we are not consumed, Because His compassions fail not. They are new every morning' Great is Your faithfulness. **[Lamentations 3:22-23]**

Who Gon' Check Me, Boo?

Yeah I admit it, I'm greedy. Who gon' check me Boo? I know my appetite is out of control. But I will not stop! I will stuff myself with the word of God until I die or until Jesus comes (whichever happens first).

Think about it. The Bible is the only real super food. It doesn't make you fat, cause disease or spoil. In fact, it removes weight, cures diseases and stays fresh from everlasting to everlasting. So have as much as you want. It does a body good!

CHEW ON THIS:
Oh, how I love Your law! It is my meditation all the day. [**Psalm 119:97**]

Paint The Barn

Many years ago, when the late, great Bible scholar J. Vernon McGee was asked if women in the church should be allowed to wear make-up, he replied, "If the barn needs paintin', paint the barn."

These days wearing make-up isn't really a big issue for Christian women. But some of us are walking around here looking like a Cover Girl on the outside with butt-ugly hearts on the inside.

Does your heart need a fresh coat or two of paint? I'd like to suggest a few colors to help you beat that thing into submission! How about Loving Lavender, Pink Patience, Righteous Red, Tenderhearted Tan or Gracious Green? Let's all get beautified from the inside-out. What other colors can you think of?

CHEW ON THIS:

Rather let it be *the hidden person of the heart, with the incorruptible* beauty *of a gentle and quiet spirit, which is very precious in the sight of God.* **[1 Peter 3:4]**

'Bout That Life

Today we hear people, especially young ones, talking about how they're "bout that life." I'll admit I'm old and I didn't know what the heck that meant. Apparently it's a way of proclaiming one's allegiance to their crew as in: "You know I'm bout that life, dawg."

Well if that's the case, Jesus was 'bout that life, too—that mercy life, that compassion life, that selfless life. That love life. He proved it on the cross when He became our sin sacrifice, when He journeyed to Hell and fought Satan for the keys to death, hell and the grave. And He rose from the dead that Sunday morning so we too can be 'bout that life now and for eternity.

Are you down?

CHEW ON THIS:

Jesus said to her, "I am the resurrection and the life, he who believes in Me will live even if he dies." And everyone who lives, and believes in Me will never die. **[John 11:25-26]**

Top of the Pops

There's a song that says, "If lovin' you is wrong I don't want to be right." Dumbest thing I've ever heard. What the song is really saying is, "If lovin' you is wrong I don't want to...live in peace and contentment. I don't care that I've compromised my intimacy with God to be intimate with my lover. I'd much rather live in a state of perpetual torment caused by guilt and shame for a few stolen moments of sensual pleasure." But I guess that version will never make it to the top of the charts.

CHEW ON THIS:

Whoever commits adultery with a woman lacks understanding; He who does so destroys his own soul. [**Proverbs 6:32**]

Miracles in the Details

Had an incredible epiphany yesterday. I realized that God knows the precise number of hairs on my head—including the ones in my wig! What an awesome God we serve. He knows the most intimate details of our lives. He is mindful of our every hurt, disappointment, frustration, and fear.

He knows things about us that we don't even know. And not only does He know, He cares.

Whatever challenge you're faced with today, you can rest in the knowledge that God is fully aware of it, and that He has supplied everything little thing you need in order to press through and emerge victoriously. His miracles are in the details.

CHEW ON THIS:

But the very hairs of your head are all numbered. Do not fear therefore; you are of more value than many sparrows.
[Luke 12:7]

Dancing with the Father

When it comes to you, God is like Patrick Swayze in the film, "Dirty Dancing." He says, "Nobody puts Baby in a corner!" So go ahead and grab His hand. Get up outta that seat and let Him lead you onto life's dance floor.

Remember to spot—meaning keep your eyes on Him to avoid getting dizzy. And don't be afraid of the lift! He's got you. Then SHINE! Let your light shine before men so they can see your good [foot]works and glory your Father in heaven.

CHEW ON THIS:

"You are the light of the world. A city that is set on a hill cannot be hidden. Nor do they light a lamp and put it under a basket, but on a lampstand, and it gives light to all who are in the house." **[Matthew 5:14-16]**

He Delivers

Sorry Ladies, I've got to call us on this one. Why is it that single women seem to be growing fatter and fatter? Could it be because we don't have a man of our own to nibble on? Is it that we're so frustrated with being on our own that we resort to spending time with whomever we can? Is that why we get with Mack...Donald's? Kick it with Carl..'s Jr.? Some of us have gotten so desperate and so sluttish that we're hanging out over at Popeye's, Arby's and Jack's. There are even those who've totally given up the ghost and said, "Forget it" and are now posted up with Wendy!

Come on Women of God, let's get it together. Time to find our comfort not in food, but in the Comforter (and I don't mean the one on your bed). The Holy Spirit is our comfort. He's open 24 hours a day and he ALWAYS delivers!

CHEW ON THIS:

"And I will pray the Father, and He will give you another Helper that He may abide with you forever." [John 14:16]

Don't Be a Seymour

Are you a Seymour? In the film "Little Shop of Horrors," mild-mannered flower shop worker Seymour finds himself doing the unthinkable to satisfy the appetite of his ravenous, flesh and blood-eating plant. In the beginning the plant was small and sort of cute. But quickly it grew into a huge monster that Seymour was unable to control. The outcome was gruesome.

In a word, that is what sin is in our lives. Gruesome. It starts out small and sort of cute. But over time it grows into a crazed killer robbing us of our very lives. Don't be a Seymour. Don't feed the plant of sin. Starve it to death while it is small. Destroy it before it destroys you.

CHEW ON THIS:

For the wages of sin is death, but the gift of God is eternal life in Christ Jesus our Lord. **[Romans 6:23]**

[205]

Eat! Taste! See!

Did you know that you were built with the capacity to accomplish all that God's called you to?

Then why are you sitting there?

Laziness will cause you to starve to death with a fridge full of food.

Now you can sit there and starve if you want to, that's on you. But don't show up in heaven looking at God all crazy when He gave you everything you need to do good works to His glory. I'm just sayin'...

CHEW ON THIS:

A lazy man buries his hand in the bowl, And will not so much as bring it to his mouth again. [**Proverbs 19:24**]

iGod

Everybody's got a tablet these days. Even my 4 year-old granddaughter, Lillian, has her own tablet. People play games, check e-mails, and read books all on a portable device meant to make communication faster, easier, more clear. But is it? Seems to me the more ways we have to talk about stuff, the more problems we see.

However, the tablet is not a new concept. In fact, God created the very first tablet when he made man. He installed a tablet in our hearts. He even provided an extensive instruction manual to show us how to operate it. It says that we are to *write kindness and truth on the tablet of our hearts*. (See Proverbs 3:3)

As we go through our day, let's make sure that kindness and truth are evident in all of our communications with one another. Write them in a BOLD font on the tablet of your heart so all the world can see your iGod.

CHEW ON THIS:

Therefore you shall lay up these words of mine in your heart and in your soul, and bind them as a sign on your hand, and they shall be as frontlets between your eyes. **[Deuteronomy 11:18]**

Dissed

In contemporary slang the word "diss" is used to show disrespect or to belittle someone, as in:

"Oh no that heifah did not just walk past me and not speak. How she gon' diss me like that?"

Yeah, you know how we do. But did you know that the word has its origins in the Latin prefix "dis" meaning "apart," "away," or "off"?

So check this out. If you're feeling…

Dis-couraged…You're apart from your courage.
Dis-contented…You're away from your contentment.
Dis-tracted…You're off track.

Begin your day by purposing in your heart to reclaim your courage, reconnect with your contentment and get your focus back on track. Don't let life "dis" you, Boo.

CHEW ON THIS:

Be strong and very courageous. Be careful to obey all the law my servant Moses gave you; do not turn from it to the right or to the left, that you may be successful wherever you go. **[Joshua 1:7]**

Be Yourself

Love is not blind. It sees beauty in the most unlovely people.

My sister-friend LaDonna is the first person I heard use the saying, "Be yourself because everyone else is taken." She spoke those words into my heart during one of the darkest periods of my life and I'm forever grateful. That simple truth set me on the path to freedom from seeking approval from others. What will it take for you to finally understand that you are more than enough just the way you are? You really are.

CHEW ON THIS:

For do I now persuade men, or God? Or do I seek to please men? For if I still pleased men, I would not be a bondservant of Christ. **[Galatians 1:10]**

Treat Yourself

If you think about it, the scriptures are a lot like those mini, powdered donuts they sell at the local convenience store. A marvel in engineering, they are perfectly symmetrical, bite-sized morsels that fit just right in the mouth. Instead of gulping them down one after another, it's more satisfying to chew them slowly, allowing all of your senses to fully enjoy the complex flavors and textures.

Others know when you've eaten a powdered donut by the telltale residue on your lips. Likewise, they can tell when you consume the scriptures on a regular basis, its sweetness clings to your life. So go head over to God's 7-11, the Bible, and get yourself a treat. It's always open.

CHEW ON THIS:

All Scripture is given by inspiration of God, and is profitable for doctrine, for reproof, for correction, for instruction in righteousness, that the man of God may be complete, thoroughly equipped for every good work.
[2 Timothy 3:16-17]

Quit Talkin' Out Yo Neck!

Done any volunteer work lately? Made a sizeable donation to a charity? Sacrificed a weekend to help a friend move? Yeah well, it's best to keep it to yourself. No need to broadcast your good deeds to the world. In fact, it was God who first said "Don't pop yo' collar. Stop tootin' your own horn. And quit talkin' out the side of yo neck?" Don't believe me? Well it's right there in Psalm 75:4-5. And I quote…

"I said to the boastful, 'Do not deal boastfully,' and the wicked, 'Do not lift up the horn. Do not lift up your horn on high; Do not speak with a stiff neck."

See, told ya. No seriously, that's what "stiff neck" means in the Hebrew text. No I'm not boasting. I'm just tellin' you what it says. LOL

CHEW ON THIS:

Take heed that you do not do your charitable deeds before men, to be seen by them. Otherwise you have no reward from your Father in heaven. **[Matthew 6:1]**

Sizzlin' For Jesus

Okay, so you ever go over to someone's house for breakfast and they serve you old bacon? At first glance it looks alright. But one bite and you can tell the bacon is old because it doesn't taste bacony anymore. Well then, let me ask you this? Is your life in Christ bacony? Or, do you just look like a Christian without having the flavor of one?

Our lives should be so tasty that it causes others to want to "taste and see that the Lord is good." So don't wait until your expiration date to get to sizzlin'! Share the love of God with someone today!

CHEW ON THIS:

You are the salt of the earth; but if the salt loses its flavor, how shall it be seasoned? It is then good for nothing but to be thrown out and trampled underfoot by men.
[Matthew 5:13]

But...

Does any of this sound familiar? "I know I should read my Bible more often Lord, but..." "I know I should spent time with you in prayer Lord, but..." "I know I should tell others about your goodness Lord, but..." Listen, it's time to quit sticking your "but" in God's face.

Either living life His way is your priority or it isn't. Please stop making excuses. It's rude and...well, you just look crazy. Imagine what your life would be if God decided to stuck a "but" in your face. Can you really imagine Him saying something like, "I know you need air to breathe my child, but..." 'Nuf said.

CHEW ON THIS:
"No one can serve two masters; for either he will hate the one and love the other, or else he will be loyal to the one and despise the other. You cannot serve God and mammon."
[Matthew 6:24]

In His Presence

Remember back in the day when we used to say that we "go with somebody" as in "I go with him; I go with her"? We'd be up all hours of the night talking on the telephone. (You sleep? Nope. I'm sleepy, but I'm not sleep.) All we wanted was to be in that person's presence, to hear their voice, and to get to know all we could about them. Then, the next day at school, all your friends wanted to know all your business. What did he say? What did she say? And you were more than happy to oblige them and tell all you found out.

So here are a few questions to ponder:

1) **Are you and God still going together?**
2) **What have you learned about Him that you didn't know a year ago? Six months ago? Two days ago?**
3) **When is the last time you told somebody else what you know about Him?**

CHEW ON THIS:

And this is eternal life, that they may know You, the only true God, and Jesus Christ whom You have sent. [**John 17:3**]

Yes And Amen

Alex Sheen is the founder of "Because I Said I Would," a non-profit dedicated to "bettering humanity through the power of a promise." The 28-year old Sheen was inspired to start the movement by the death of his father. After his dad's passing he remembers trying to recall a single promise that his father had failed to keep. He couldn't.

His father was a man of his word. And so is ours. Our heavenly Father is not a man who can lie. He is truth personified. As we meditate on the promises He's made to us in scripture we can rest assured that He will make good on every last one of them. "For all the promises of God find their Yes in him. That is why it is through him that we utter our Amen to God for his glory." (2 Corinthians 1:20)

CHEW ON THIS:
God is not a man, that He should lie, Nor a son of man, that He should repent. Has He said and will He not do it? Or has He spoken, and will He not make it good? **[Numbers 23:19]**

Spice It Up!

You say your life is bland? You say you're tired of you going through life, day after day, month after month, year after agonizing year, just hoping to make it through to the next vacation, payday or even the next crisis? You say you're longing for something to shake up the mundaneness of your existence?

Well step right folks! God has got just what you need. Because he wants you to experience a tasty life, he's created a special seasoning to help you kick it up a notch. Try patented "God's Spice of Life." It's flavorful blend of goodness, grace, mercy, kindness, forgiveness, patience, faithfulness, and peace. Stir it into your life and enjoy!

CHEW ON THIS:

"I have come that you might have life, and that you might have it more abundantly." **[John 10:10]**

A Light in the Darkness

In Michael Jackson's video, *Billie Jean,* he danced along a darkened sidewalk. However, each time Michael took a step forward, all of a sudden the section of sidewalk beneath him would light up. That is what studying the Bible does for us.

As we meditate on God's word it becomes a lamp unto our feet and a light unto our path illuminating the way we should go *one step at a time*. Uncertain of which direction you should go? Step into the scriptures and let them be your guiding light.

CHEW ON THIS:
Your word is a lamp to my feet and a light to my path. [**Psalm 119:105**]

The Secret Password

You had to be creative if you wanted to get drunk during Prohibition. Some people brewed their own booze in the bathtub (yuck). Others frequented speakeasies, a sort of bar on the down low. To get in, one had to give a password at the door. The secret code was always something like "Rocco sent me." Rocco's name had clout. The very mention of it would cause the door to open.

Our password is the name of Jesus. Believing on His name gains us entry into the very throne room of God. When you evoke the name of Jesus in prayer, it causes the heavenly doors to fling open because His name has clout with God. Once you get in you can drink as much as you want. Not fire water, but living water. And here's the best part...IT'S FREE!

So go ahead, knock on God's door. And tell Him that Jesus sent you.

CHEW ON THIS:

"And He said to me, "It is done! I am the Alpha and the Omega, the Beginning and the End. I will give of the fountain of the water of life freely to him who thirsts."
[Revelations 21:6]

Bedside Baptist

Do you regularly attend Bedside Baptist where the Pastor Pillow presides? Do you consider watching TV or online ministries as "getting it in?" News flash! YouTube ain't fellowship.

YouTube can't pray for you, baptize you or stand with you in times of trouble. Let something jump off in your life, then try calling YouTube for help and see what happens.

So get up out that bed you lazy lima bean! Find a church, an in-home fellowship, a lunchtime prayer meeting, a campus Bible study or somethin'! Your destiny is linked to people, not your pillow.

CHEW ON THIS:

"...not forsaking the assembling of ourselves together, as is the manner of some, but exhorting one another, and so much the more as you see the Day approaching." [Hebrews 10:25]

God's To-Do List

I doubt that of all the things God has on his to-do list today, hiding His will for your life is one of them. But an occasional reading of scripture is not going to cut it if you truly want to know God's will. If you're desperate for divine direction then you've got to set aside time to meditate, contemplate, ruminate, evaluate, percolate and, yes, even regurgitate the word of God—the Bible. The answers to your questions are there. Seek and you SHALL find them.

CHEW ON THIS:

"Apply your heart to instruction, and your ears to words of knowledge."
[Proverbs 23:12]

God's Not Deaf!

Do you ever wonder sometimes if God needs a hearing aid? I mean you've asked him for an answer to that problem like a million times. Yet he still doesn't answer. Well, it's not that God has a hearing problem. We have a listening problem. We go on and on like Charlie Brown's teacher, "Waa waa waa waa." Meanwhile, God waits patiently for a chance to get "his Word" in edgewise. Want answers? Quiet your soul and wait in silence for the hope that is in him.

CHEW ON THIS:
It is *good that* one *should hope and wait quietly for the salvation of the Lord.*
[Lamentations 3:26]

Get "The Works"

Ever notice how your car just seems to run better after its been washed? Especially if you get "The Works." Our lives are like that too. Want your life to "run better?" Detail it with the Word of God.

First, soap it up with the suds of God's love and forgiveness. Let it give you a high-pressure, spot-free rinse to remove the droppings of sin. Then, allow it to dry your tears, apply the sealer wax of grace, and finish it all off with the sweet fragrance of Christ.

CHEW ON THIS:

"Now thanks be to God who always leads us in triumph in Christ, and through us diffuses the fragrance of His knowledge in every place. For we are to God the fragrance of Christ among those who are being saved and among those who are perishing." **[2 Corinthians 2:14-15]**

Born-Again Killer

If you remember the movie, "Children of the Corn," you'll recall that it was about a bunch of creepy kids who killed all of the grown-ups in the village. But did you know that as "Children of the King," we too have a license to kill? No seriously, I'm not making this stuff up. Read it for yourself: "For if you live by its dictates, you will die. But if through the power of the spirit you put to death the deeds of your sinful nature, you will live."

In other words, if you're a follower of Christ, you are a born killer. Or I should say, a "born-again" killer. So go ahead, slash the sin in your life. Bludgeon that rebellion. Poison that pride. Just don't be all creepy about it. You'll freak people out.

CHEW ON THIS:

And those who are Christ's have crucified the flesh with its passions and desires.
[Galatians 5:24]

Congratulations

"To reflect on your blessings is to rehearse God's accomplishments." —Max Lucado

When's the last time you congratulated God for His accomplishments? Have you ever said to Him, "That sun and moon thing? Brilliant!" Ever consider saying, "God, you ROCK!"?

Giving God a thumb's up may sound sort of silly, but actually it's a powerful way of expressing gratitude for all He's done. Purpose in your heart each day to think about something God has done for you. Then give Him a high-5! He deserves at least that.

Remember: God is not just "the rock," GOD ROCKS!

CHEW ON THIS:

You alone are the Lord; You have made heaven, The heaven of heavens, with all their host, The earth and everything on it, The seas and all that is in them, And You preserve them all. The host of heaven worships You. **[Nehemiah 9:6]**

An Order of Wings, Please

I love Wing Stop. Yeah, I said it. I love those crispy, greezee (not greasy, but greezee) and gelatinous bits of chicken flesh all covered in sodium-rich lemon pepper seasoning. Truth be told, the place should be called, Wings "Make-Your-Heart" Stop.

But there are some other wings that I love even more. They're actually large enough and strong enough to cover me. They provide a secret hiding place when I'm troubled by the death and destruction in the world around me. These wings are my refuge and my fortress. In the shadow of these wings I don't have to be afraid because I know I am safe.

Should you, by some chance, find yourself frightened of the terror by night and the arrows that fly by day, I invite you to join me in the shadow of the wings of the Almighty. There's plenty of room. And these wings won't stop your heart. They will protect it.

CHEW ON THIS:
He shall cover you with His feathers,
And under His wings you shall take refuge.
[Psalm 91:4]

Get Gangsta

I ain't gonna lie to you it's been a rough week. Several times I've been tempted to slap the snot out of someone. Seems this person was on a mission to get on my last nerve. You know the type—self-centered, spoiled and ungrateful. They think the world revolves around them, and they get all bent all out of shape when things don't go their way. I mean this person's constant ingratitude 'bout wore me out!

Finally I snapped! I had to step to her and go straight gangsta. I didn't care who heard me either. I stood right there in front of my bathroom mirror and I told myself, "Look! I'm sick of listening to you complain. Either be grateful for what you DO have or SHUT UP!"

Sometimes you just gotta get gangsta and "check yo self before you wreck yo self." The only way to correct a bad attitude is to give yourself a good talking to—even if people think you're nuts.

CHEW ON THIS:

Therefore, since we are receiving a kingdom which cannot be shaken, let us have grace, by which we may serve God acceptably with reverence and godly fear. **[Hebrews 12:28]**

He Did That

This morning I'm thinking of my dear sister-friend, Stephanie, who has a unique way of complimenting you. Whether it's a new outfit you're wearing or a dish you brought to the potluck, when Stephy says, "You did that!" you know she's impressed. "You did that" is her way of congratulating you on a job well done.

Likewise when I think of the awesomeness of God's handiwork I'm inclined to say, "Lord, you did that!" From the sound of rain falling, the giggles of my grandchildren, flowers, rainbows, trees, clouds, animals or the different shades of skin that folks come in, God's creativity overwhelms me. And to think, he did all that for us to enjoy.

I hope you'll take time to stop for a moment today, turn off the TV, get out of the house and simply admire the work of God's hand. He did that...just for you!

CHEW ON THIS:
O Lord, how manifold are Your works!
In wisdom You have made them all.
The earth is full of Your possessions.
[Psalm 104:24]

LATE NIGHT MENU

The Lord will command His loving kindness in

the daytime, And in the night His song shall *be*

with me—A prayer to the God of my life.

[Psalm 42:8]

Guest Check

CHECK NO.
6436-17

TABLE NO. | NO. PERSONS | SERVER NO.

Scrambled Eggs	$3.85
Orange Juice	$1.25
Prayer	FREE

TAX
TOTAL

Thank you! Come again.

Booty Shorts and All

You ain't got to wash the stamp off your hand, brush the Hennessy off your tongue or change out your red bottoms just to go into the house of the Lord. Jesus saw you at the club last night and He ain't trippin'. Come just as you are because you are loved just as you are—booty shorts and all! (Just be prepared because the Mother's Board is about to throw a clothes drive in your honor.) But Jesus, He ain't trippin'. See you Sunday!

CHEW ON THIS:

All that the Father gives Me will come to Me, and the one who comes to Me I will by no means cast out. [John 6:37]

The Green Eyes Of God

I read an article on a dating website the other day that, quite frankly, made my skin crawl. It encouraged women to "tone down the God stuff" in order to attract men. It was explained that some men are "turned off" by open displays of worship.

Now Ladies, I want you to listen carefully to Auntie T. Faye for a minute. There should NEVER be a man in your life placed above the Creator of your life. "Toning down" one's passion for God in order to be more palatable to another human being is not only nonsense, its dangerous nonsense. To desire to please a man more than you desire to honor God will ultimately cost you your spiritual life (and maybe even your physical one).

Any man who is embarrassed by or, more likely, intimidated by a woman's outwardly expression of love for her Lord has some soul searching to do. Ask yourself: Do I want to live with a brown-eyed man or a green-eyed God?

CHEW ON THIS:

But seek first the kingdom of God and His righteousness, and all these things shall be added to you. [**Matthew 6:33**]

Get Lost!

You ever wonder why single men stay away from the church in droves? Because as soon as one of them hits the door, single sisters start eyeballing him like he's the last pork chop at a Baptist potluck.

Then there's always that one sister who goes as far as to "name and claim" him, talkin' 'bout "The Lord told me he's the one." What makes you think the Lord's gonna tell you and not him? The Bible says let a thing be established by two or three witnesses. I'm sure He didn't mean you and the voices in your head.

The word says "He who finds a wife..." The optimum word here is "finds." Do yourselves a favor, Ladies—get lost!

CHEW ON THIS:
He who finds a wife finds a good thing, And obtains favor from the Lord. [Proverbs 18:22]

Hands Up!

Masturbation issues? Hands lifted in praise are less likely to wander down under. Let God put your soul under arrest. Get those hands up where HE can see them.

#RealTalkForGrownChristians
#NotYourMama'sDevotional
#SomebodyJustPutThisBookBackOnTheShelf
#SomebodyJustPickedItBackUpAgain
#MyTopicalBibleSkippedThisSubject
#SmileAndLookStraightAhead
#BeCelibateOnPurpose

CHEW ON THIS:

Or do you not know that your body is the temple of the Holy Spirit who is in you, whom you have from God, and you are not your own? For you were bought at a price; therefore glorify God in your body and in your spirit, which are God's.
[1 Corinthians 6:19-20]

All's I'm Sayin'

Uh oh! Brace yourselves. I feel a rant coming on! And here it is: I am sooooo sick and tired of racism within the body of Christ. How can the right hand be prejudiced against the left hand? Can't we all just get along?

How about we start close to home—in the Bible bookstores. Talk about the next to last bastion of legalized segregation (Hollywood is the last. But that's another rant for another day). In the music department of most Bible bookstores you'll find signage that reads: Urban Gospel. Translation = Black gospel artists. Now this could be construed as progress especially since up until a few years ago signs blatantly read: "Black Gospel." We've come a long way Baby...not.

Shouldn't the categories be based on the genre not the color of the artist's epidermis? I'm just sayin'! There are plenty soulful Caucasian artists like Gary Oliver and Danny Chambers who have as much so called "urban" cred as many Black artists. Shouldn't they share shelf space with Kirk Franklin and 'nem? By the same token shouldn't more traditional worship singers like Larnelle Harris and Wintley Phipps move on up to the Eastside to the deluxe section of Worship Music alongside their more straight-laced and usually White counterparts?

All's I'm sayin' is (Yes, I said "all's") that it's time to tear down the walls of racism in our own backyard before we go preaching inclusion to the world.

Okay, I'm done.

CHEW ON THIS:

For as many of you as were baptized into Christ have put on Christ. There is neither Jew nor Greek, there is neither slave nor free, there is neither male nor female; for you are all one in Christ Jesus. [Galatians 3:27-28]

The Wildman and the Colored Woman

Today I visited Wildman's Civil War Surplus Store in Downtown Kennesaw, Georgia where I spent time chatting with its owner, self-proclaimed "power honky," Dent Myers. Bearded, bandana'd, and packing a loaded pistol on each hip, the wooly yet warm Dent is as much of a curiosity as his overstuffed store and the Confederate memorabilia it contains.

Stocked to the rafters with rare books, antique guns, swords, uniforms, Sambo dolls and all sorts of whatnots from the Civil War era through Reconstruction, the windowless storefront was stifling. Still, I couldn't tear myself away.

After paying the admission price of 25 cents to step into the museum (a back room cordoned off with a chain), I stepped into a world nothing could have prepared me for. One long counter displayed a variety of Nazi paraphernalia—which was disconcerting enough. But then, I made a sharp right turn and suddenly came face-to-face with a mannequin dressed in a stained and yellowed Klansman robe and hood. A handwritten note that read: "1920's New England" was pinned to its faded sash. Hanging loosely around the neck of the mustached dummy was a bullwhip and two thick ropes, each tied into a noose.

My visceral reaction was quick and unexpected. Hot tears battered my eyes, my stomach rushed into my throat, and the last vestiges of the air in my lungs was knocked clean out of me. I became that Black washer woman who dared to speak her piece; that young Black man whose eyes rested too long upon the flesh of a White woman, and the child whose father mysteriously disappeared in the night. For a moment, and only a moment, I knew for the first time in my life the type of fear that is only spawned by hatred.

But instead of fleeing, I allowed love to rise. Soon the wild man Confederate from Dixie and the wild-haired "colored" comedy writer from up North were able to find common ground on which to exchange genuine pleasantries about life, love and legacies. Hatred lost that day.

CHEW ON THIS:

Let love be without hypocrisy. Abhor what is evil. Cling to what is good. **[Romans 12:9]**

God's Most Wanted

Many are on the verge of committing a spiritual felony. They are walking around with their finger on the temper trigger ready to pull it at the slightest provocation. They are armed and dangerous with thoughts like: "Just let that heifah say one more rude thing to me." Or "I can't wait to tell that chump what I really think about him."

Well, before you snap and splatter someone's brain matter all to kingdom come, remember what Proverbs says: "A fool is quick-tempered, but a wise person stays calm when insulted." Yeah, I know. It's hard. But still, the next time somebody ticks you off, keep calm and carry on!

CHEW ON THIS:
For wrath kills a foolish man, And envy slays a simple one. [**Job 5:2**]

Just the Facts, Ma'am

Fact is, a fact is only information until the truth of that fact becomes indisputably evident. For example: You're in a sexual relationship with a person who is not your spouse. That's information. Until a marriage covenant takes place that's all you have—information.

Commitment makes a marriage fact. Fidelity makes it a fact. A union blessed of God makes that information fact. So get out that bed and go get yo' facts straight! Remember: God is the ultimate judge and He'll be looking at the facts.

CHEW ON THIS:

Marriage is honorable among all, and the bed undefiled; but fornicators and adulterers God will judge. [**Hebrews 13:4**]

That's A Helluva Thing To Say!

"Go to Hell!" "WTH" "Who the hell do you think you are?" are?" "Man, that job is a living hell."

How does reading these common phrases make you feel? Uncomfortable? Offended? Or did you chuckle? Now ask yourself, why. Perhaps it made you think of someone, (even yourself). There is a reason the "h-e-double toothpicks" word causes a visceral response in most people. Could it be that it's because instinctually we know hell is a real place?

No, this isn't meant to be a dissertation on the existence of hell. But do consider this: Words have creative power. God spoke the universe into being. It is written that the power of life and death is in the tongue. So, if words contain creative power and you tell someone to "Go to hell" then... Yeah, uh huh, exactly.

CHEW ON THIS:

A good man out of the good treasure of his heart brings forth good things, and an evil man out of the evil treasure brings forth evil things. **[Matthew 12:35]**

Real Talk

(Warning: Do NOT read this if you're a person who is easily offended or who believes Christians should not discuss certain topics publicly.)

Single Ladies listen to Auntie T. Faye. A man's member is like a genie in a bottle. If you rub it, something will appear. So if you're out on a date and find yourself in the clinches just remember this: Consequence is the constant companion of compromise. Think with your head, not your hormones. And keep your hand to yourself (At least until there's a ring on it). Let's keep it holy out there!

CHEW ON THIS:

God's will is for you to be holy, so stay away from all sexual sin. Then each of you will control his own body and live in holiness and honor.
[1 Thessalonians 4:4-5]

What Are You Selling?

The Church of Scientology scored big during the 2014 Super Bowl (even if the Broncos didn't). They received a ton of press about a commercial they ran during the break. Beautifully shot with an intriguing message, it reportedly cost the infamous religious organization 8 million dollars for sixty seconds. All sorts of commentary popped off on social media about the price tag. The loudest among the critics were Christians.

But why?

Why give a rip about how Tom Cruise, John Travolta and 'nem choose to spend their money? Instead of railing against what another religion is doing or not doing, how about training your focus on what we, as followers of Christ, are doing or not doing?

As disciples we are walking, talking commercials for Jesus Christ. We are the only advertisement he has. So the question is not: Why would the Church of Scientology spend all that money when there are homeless people needing shelter and hungry children needing food? The question is: What are you promoting, Christian? When people look at sixty seconds, sixty days or sixty years of your life what do they see? Are you promoting patience, joy, or forgiveness? Are you demonstrating a new and improved you that lives in complete peace and total freedom? Does your life make people want to rush right out and buy what you're "selling?"

Let's stop picking at the Witnesses and the Scientologists and the Mormons and the little bald-headed people at the airport. They are simply taking their role as pitchmen seriously.

CHEW ON THIS:

We are therefore Christ's ambassadors, as though God were making his appeal through us. We implore you on Christ's behalf: Be reconciled to God.
[2 Corinthians 5:20]

Big Mouth

Did you know that the word "gossip" means to "be open, wide, spacious"? In other words, a gossip is nothing more than someone with a BIG mouth.

Proverbs 20:19 instructs us to not even associate with a gossip. Gossip, slander and murmuring can create drama. It can drive a permanent wedge between even the closest of friends. Don't get caught up! Here's a little something to keep you on point.

Five Keys to Living Gossip-Free

1) If you wouldn't share the story in the presence of those who are in the story, don't share it.

2) If you find yourself whispering while sharing a story (and you're not in a movie theater), you're probably gossiping. Stop it.

3) If you don't want it told, don't tell it.

4) Ask yourself who is to benefit from you sharing the story? And be honest.

5) Tell the story out loud to Jesus before you tell anyone else and see how it feels. Conviction is the best barometer.

CHEW ON THIS:

A talebearer reveals secrets, But he who is of a faithful spirit conceals a matter.
[Proverbs 11:13]

All Dog(ma)s Don't Go to Heaven

I'll admit I had some trepidation about including this bite of manna. It seems that whenever you mention the word "dogma" people generally and singularly think of Christianity. So before I continue, please allow me to refresh our collective memories about what the word means.

dog•ma /dôgmə/noun: a principle or set of principles laid down by an authority as incontrovertibly true.

(synonyms: teaching, tenet, principle, precept, maxim, article of faith, canon, creed, credo, set of beliefs, doctrine, ideology)

With that said, and if all hearts and minds are clear on the definition, I just have one thing to say:

Some dogmas need to be caught and put down because they are running around out there giving people spiritual rabies!

I'm not even talking about other religions. I'm talking about the diseased dogmas that have attacked the Body of Christ. Early-stage symptoms include confusion and apathy. Left untreated spiritual rabies will ultimately lead to death. Known causes include the teaching of a watered down, materialistic and/or hyper-legalistic version of the Gospel message.

If you suspect that you been infected by false teaching, triple your dosage of personal Bible study immediately. It's one of the few prescription medications without harmful side effects that will blind you, give you a rash or shut your kidneys down.

CHEW ON THIS:

"...Guard what was committed to your trust, avoiding the profane and idle babblings and contradictions of what is falsely called knowledge—by professing it some have strayed concerning the faith..."
[1 Timothy 6:20-21]

SEASONAL FAVORITES

Praise the Lord! Oh, give thanks to the Lord,

for He is good! For His mercy endures forever.

[Psalm 106:1]

Try our Red, White & Blue Plate Special

God Keep "U.S."

Unofficially the song "God Bless America" has replaced "The Star Spangled Banner" as our national anthem. But as beautiful as the song is, and for all of the flag waving it inspires during the patriotic holidays, its message does seem a bit redundant. The reality is that God has already blessed America abundantly. Yes, there is much to be desired about our government, culture, education and healthcare systems, still if we had to choose between living here and somewhere like Malawi, I don't think it would be a hard decision.

America has more going for it than against it. But the growing ingratitude we show for our many blessings poses a threat to the favor God has shown this country. So how about a new song? A song that calls for us to collectively humble ourselves, seek His face and pray. Instead of "God Bless America" how about "God Keep U.S."

CHEW ON THIS:

"...if My people who are called by My name will humble themselves, and pray and seek My face, and turn from their wicked ways, then I will hear from heaven, and will forgive their sin and heal their land." **[2 Chronicles 7:14]**

The 85¢ Blessing

Today I got a check for a whopping 85¢. It's payment for the re-airing of a television show I wrote back in the 90's. Receiving these residual payments from the WGA (Writers Guild of America) is always a welcome, if not ironic, surprise.

I think back on the grueling 10-14 hour production days, the temperamental stars, missed moments in the lives of my young sons, the crushing blow of cancellation and the mad scrabble for the next gig.

And for what? 85¢ (Well, that's one way of looking at it.)

After more than 25 years in the business, the big paying gigs are now few and far between. Yet, I am still very grateful. A check for less than a buck may be an insult to some. But in some third world countries there are entire families who eat on less than 85¢ a day.

So while I would've loved to receive money that folds, I'll take the kind that jingles gladly. It serves as a reminder of how God has kept me over the years, and how He continues to bless me in small ways each and every day. Now if you'll excuse me, I've got a check to deposit.

CHEW ON THIS:

I know how to be abased, and I know how to abound. Everywhere and in all things I have learned both to be full and to be hungry, both to abound and to suffer need. I can do all things through Christ who strengthens me. **[Philippians 4:12-13]**

Christmas Time is Here

That's Nice

As I write, there is exactly 57 days, 21 hours, 48 minutes and 21 seconds until Christmas. Kids around the world are beginning to clean up their act in anticipation. Now, I won't ask if you've been naughty or nice, but I will ask you to consider this: Have you been "nice" or "kind?" Until recently I always thought the words were synonymous. But that little assumption got called into question recently when I heard someone pray these words: "God, teach us to be kind, not just nice." I've since learned that "nice" is how we describe people and things when there's no apparent defect ("That's a nice car" or "Starnisha's new boo seems nice").

I've come to understand that a person can do nice things and still have an evil heart. In my old neighborhood there was a group of gangbangers who took a break from their illegal activities twice a year to organize a Mother's Day brunch and a Christmas toy drive. Was it a nice thing to do? Absolutely. Were these thugs kind? Sorry, but no.

Here's the deal. Kindness is a condition of the heart. It's not something you put on and take off at will. Kindness, by its very nature, is a fruit of the Holy Spirit. And this fruit means that one is not just useful, but useful, gentle, and pleasant. Kindness is permanently affixed to love. They always work in tandem and cannot be separated. So the next time you do something nice, ask yourself: Am I being kind or just nice? Is this an act of love or just an act? Ho! Ho! Ho!

CHEW ON THIS:

And be kind to one another, tenderhearted, forgiving one another, even as God in Christ forgave you. **[Ephesians 4:32]**

I Love Ya Tomorrow

There's a weird phenomenon that occurs every year around the holiday season—the number of deaths among the famous and celebrated skyrockets. It has yet to be explained. But it always elicits the same reaction. Upon hearing the news of a sudden death of a public figure we find ourselves contemplating our own mortality. We encourage one another to "live life to the fullest," to make each day count because it may be our last. Choruses of "tomorrow isn't promised" ring out almost as loudly as Christmas carols.

But while we should strive to lead productive lives, it should not be with the pall of fatalism hanging over it.

Truth is, tomorrow IS promised. The Bible is clear—our time in the earthly realm is limited. Yet our existence is unlimited. Whether we spent our next day here or in the presence of our Lord, we will surely have a tomorrow.

If I could rewrite that famous Broadway show tune it would go a little something like this: "Tomorrow. Tomorrow. I love ya' tomorrow. You're already here today!"

Let's live each day with eternity in our hearts, rejoicing in the day and for the days to come. For in Christ there will always be a tomorrow.

CHEW ON THIS:

And many of those who sleep in the dust of the ground will awake, these to everlasting life, but the others to disgrace and everlasting contempt. [Daniel 12:2]

Behind Closed Doors

During the holidays it's natural that we turn our hearts and minds towards our circle of family and friends. How easy it is for us to forget those in need—especially those who are out of sight.

All around us behind the closed doors of dwellings nearby and far away, there are families with children and senior citizens going without the basic necessities. I've recently adopted a new practice, one that I will continue throughout the year. It is simply this: For every bite I take, I will find a way for someone else to take two.

I encourage you to search your heart for ways to help put an end to hunger in America.

CHEW ON THIS:

"But if anyone has the world's goods and sees his brother in need, yet closes his heart against him, how does God's love abide in him? Little children, let us not love in word or talk but in deed and in truth." [1 John 3:17-18]

Believe

For all of its commerciality you have to admit that there is something rather beautiful about the mall during the Christmas season. The sight of twinkling lights and the sound over the PA system of Johnny Mathis crooning, "Chestnuts roasting on an open fire..." can be quite heartwarming.

Macy's is especially beautiful at this time of year with an entire department devoted to all things Christmas. I am particularly intrigued by their holiday marketing campaign slogan: "BELIEVE." Banners emblazoned with the word hang throughout the store. But for all of its beauty the slogan is sadly ambiguous.

Believe? In what?

Believe in the extra 20% off during the Early Bird doorbuster sale? Believe in the new line of Michael Kors handbags or JLo's latest fragrance? Believe in the interest that compounds on your charge-a-plate long after the Christmas is in the compost pile?

Thankfully, there is something (rather someone) more concrete for us to believe in, not only at Christmas but all year-round. We can believe that Mary's babe, the lowly Christ child, born in a manger grew into manhood. We can believe that He laid down His life on the cross in exchange for ours. We can believe that He fought death, hell and the grave to buy back our eternal freedom. And we can believe that anyone who confesses this belief with their mouth and believes it in their heart will be saved. Now that is a beautiful thing.

CHEW ON THIS:

You believe that there is one God. You do well. Even the demons believe—and tremble! **[James 2:19]**

Uh Oh! Your Ignorance Is Showing

The trailer for Tyler Perry's Christmas-themed film depicts the outrageous character Madea telling a group of schoolchildren the story of the birth of Christ. She tells them, "The baby Jesus was born to the Virgin Mary...J. Blige." That's nonsense and foolishness, of course. But it's comedy and a very funny line to cover our lack of understanding of scripture.

Listen, there's no harm in saying that you don't know. No one will fault you if you say, "Let me get back to you on that." But to piece together facts and fiction and try and pass it off as truth, well, it makes you look as crazy as Madea. As they say, it's better to remain silent and let others think you're a fool than to open your mouth and remove all doubt.

CHEW ON THIS:

Be diligent to present yourself approved to God, a worker who does not need to be ashamed, rightly dividing the word of truth.
[2 Timothy 2:15]

Eat To Edify

The beginning of a new year always inspires people to make resolutions to lose weight. Millions of dollars are spent in the month of January alone on programs, pills, powders and pre-packaged portions. But most people fall off the wagon before the Valentine's Day candy hits the shelves. (I stand accused.) So it's no surprise that resolutions rarely bring resolve.

This year I didn't bother to make a resolution. I didn't have to. God made one for me. His word reminds me that as ambassador for Christ, I have a responsibility to be temperate in all things— to show moderation and practice self-restraint. I am to discipline my body and bring it into subjection. Otherwise I am disqualified to preach to others. WOW!

And so it is for all preachers, teachers, evangelists, apostles, and anyone who has been called to share the gospel of Jesus Christ. If we are overweight for any reason other than a medical condition, we are out of order. (Oh and by the way, every believer is called to share the gospel. So that includes you. OUCH!)

Here's the deal, how can we challenge

someone to put down crack when we can't put down the Cracker Jack? Okay so there are no scriptures that say we can't eat an 8-piece combo with fries and honey mustard from Wing Stop. But seriously, how does fried chicken improve our quality of lives?

All things are lawful for us, but not all things are helpful for our bodies. So let's begin to eat to edify. Let's not gorge, but glorify. Whatever we eat or drink let's do it all to the glory of God. No, it won't be easy. But it is most necessary. The world is watching. Let's be a reflection of our Lord Jesus—fit and fabulous. I'll pray for you. Please pray for me.

CHEW ON THIS:
But I discipline my body and bring it into subjection, lest, when I have preached to others, I myself should become disqualified.
[1 Corinthians 9:27]

The One-Word Prayer

The simplicity of communicating with God is mind blowing. Ask and receive. Seek and find. He's even devised an efficient way for us to pray for the salvation and deliverance of our loved ones; a method that only requires one word—Hosanna.

The word has fallen out of favor in modern Christianity. You rarely hear anyone use it outside of the occasional hymn or Kirk Franklin joint. But contained within these seven letters is a powerful prayer that God responds to, for it is no question that it is His will—Hosanna—literally meaning, "Save now, I pray."

It is His will that all men be saved. When is the last time, if ever, that you cried out, "Hosanna"? Wait no longer. Now is the time. Over the life of that son who is battling drug and alcohol addiction, cry out, Hosanna! Over the life of that wife who's lost in the valley of depression, cry out, Hosanna! Over the life of that co-worker who tries to hide the cuts and bruises, cry out, Hosanna! Over your own life cry out! Hosanna God! Save now, I pray oh God! Save now! Cry out and see the salvation of the Lord.

CHEW ON THIS:

Therefore I exhort first of all that supplications, prayers, intercessions, and giving of thanks be made for all men, for kings and all who are in authority, that we may lead a quiet and peaceable life in all godliness and reverence. For this is good and acceptable in the sight of God our Savior, who desires all men to be saved and to come to the knowledge of the truth.
[1 Timothy 2:1-4]

What Will You Cast At His Feet?

When Jesus made his final entry into Jerusalem it was like Superman swooping in just before a plane crashes into the mountain. He got there just in the nick of time. Jerusalem was a hot bed of political and religious nonsense and foolishness. Temple prostitution was turning good business. Merchants had turned the temple into a Swap Meet. Jerusalem was not a safe place for those who believed that Jesus' declaration that he was the Messiah. Persecution was brutal. [We think we've been persecuted when a co-worker calls us a Bible thumper…Ha!]

Believing that their only hope had arrived the people shouted, Save now! Take control of this place! Then, they cast palms branches at his feet. The branches symbolized victory. But they also symbolized a high thing, an exalted thing—a thing of value or worth. But that day, they were cast at the feet of Jesus as the people asked him to take his place as Lord and king over their lives.

THE QUESTION IS: WHAT WILL YOU CAST AT THE FEET OF JESUS?

What relationship are you staying in longer than you should have because you're afraid to cast it at His feet and allow Him to Lord over your heart?

What personality trait have you relaxed into instead of casting it at Jesus' feet and allowing Him to Lord over your character? You know the one that you defend by saying, "I know I've got an attitude. That's just the way I am."

What job or business or ministry did you enter into without asking God first; the one that you're now killing yourself trying to make it work because you're trying to save your investment and or reputation?

Let Jesus save the day for you. Cast your palms at his feet and let Him rule and reign over your life.

CHEW ON THIS:
But we are to "Know that the LORD is God..." [Psalm 100:3]

The Last Will and Testament Of Christ

If there had been a reading of Jesus' will, it may have sounded something like this:

To my Father in heaven, I bequeath my spirit. To my closest friend John, I leave the responsibility of caring for the needs of my mother, Mary. To the Roman soldiers at Calvary, I leave the remaining remnants of my garments to be divided among them. To Joseph of Arimethea, I leave my body for burial. And to my faithful disciples, my devoted followers, those who believe that I am the Son of God, those who believe I laid down my life in exchange for theirs and that I will rise again, I leave my peace.

His peace. Perfect peace. Peace that passes all understanding. A peace that lacks nothing and requires nothing more than that we keep our thoughts set on Him. This is our inheritance.

Of all the things he could have left us, why did Jesus leave us "peace?" Because he knew there would be times in our lives when nothing less than his calm-in-the-middle-of-a-storm kind of peace would keep us in the midst of our trials.

Have you claimed your inheritance?

CHEW ON THIS:

"I have told you these things so that in me you may have peace. In this world you will have trouble; but take heart (be of good cheer, have joy, be at peace) I have overcome the world." **[John 16:33]**

Take-Out Menu
A NOTE FROM THE AUTHOR

Well Diners, we're at the end. I pray you've enjoyed breaking bread together here at the kitchen table. By now you should be full as a tick from feasting on the truth of God's word. I know that some of the manna has been a little tough to chew, but it is still good for us. Before you go, I just want to leave you with this last little bite:

There are no grey areas in God. You're either in or out; hot or cold. You're either living in faith or living in fear. You either serve Him or you don't; you'll either surrender your life to Him or you won't. But please know that life is short. Tomorrow isn't promised. No one can afford to continue to futz around when it comes to the final destination of the soul.

If you have not made a firm decision to give your life Jesus Christ, make today the day that you make up your mind to invite Him into your heart; to take control of your life. It's real easy. First, just believe that He is who He says He is and then just ask Him. It's as simple as that. I promise you that you'll never regret it. And your life will never be the same!

And for those of you who may have given your life to Christ already, but find yourselves slippin' and dippin', there's no shame in the game. (Trust me I've been there.) But it is time to either HANG ON OR HANG UP! God spits out the lukewarm. So come on home fam. He's waiting with open arms.

I would love to hear from you about how *Morning Manna* has encouraged you. Please take a moment to visit the website www.morningmannathebook.com and leave me a private message. Your message will be strictly confidential.

It's been an honor and a privilege to serve you! I hope you'll allow me to do it again sometime. Until then, please remember that God cares about you and so do I.

Your Server,
T. Faye

Acknowledgements

God, my Father, I am nothing without you. I can do nothing without you. And I want nothing but you. Thank you for entrusting me to share your heart and your humor and for providing everything necessary to do so.

Blessed am I to have been raised by two very strong women of God—both noted Bible teachers in their own right. Each of them taught me to reverence God and the importance of "rightly dividing the word of truth." They pointed the way. God bless and rest my mothers, Audria Mae Buckner and Lillian Marie McGehee.

My three heartbeats Brandy, V.J., and Jonathan, there is nothing I can accomplish in this life that will ever top being your Mom. I love you more than tongue can tell. Thank you for always being a source of laughter, inspiration and hope. (And thank you for Lillian, Isaiah and Dylan).

Bucky's Girls, I could not have designed a more perfect set of beautiful and brilliant sisters had I tried. Carmen, Robin (Jo), Audria (Snak), Toni and Paradise, my love for you is beyond love. Thank you for loving me back.

Sometimes God uses the eyes of others to help you see what's right in front of them. Melodie Cochran, you have always been those eyes for me. Thank you for kicking me out of your car that day. It saved my life. You're the best BFF ever!

To my BIG brothers in comedy and personal

cheer squad, Lamont "Monty B. Sharpton" Bonman, thank you for keeping the paddles ready on those occasions when I flat-lined. You are my God-send. Adam Christing, you not only unlocked the portal to my second chance, but you blew it off the hinges! Thank you for showing me how to go from "Ha Ha" to "Aha!" I am forever grateful.

To my velvet-whip of a mentor Terri McFaddin Solomon, I am better because you refused to allow me to settle.

I've been privileged to have the pastoral covering of three anointed couples. I bless the Lord for sending me champions in the form of Pastor Philip and Holly Wagner (Oasis Church LA), Pastor Frank and P. Bunny Wilson (New Dawn Christian Village) and Pastors Alex and Kai Pineda (Kingdom House of Worship).

Kingdom House of Worship, you already know what it is! You're rockin' this thing for real. Thank you for not just doing church, but for being the church. (Acts 2:42)

Every writer needs a Superhero. I've got two! One is Chicago's finest—Tiffany Thomas, you are a force to be reckoned with! My respect for you is immense and my love grows on the daily-for real, for real. The crowdfunding campaign would not have happened as it did without your magic. My other Super-Shero wears crazy glasses, is an award-winning author, entrepreneur and the best editor in reality TV. Tondra TaJuan "TeeJ" Mercer, besides inspiring me to dream again, you have consistently put your hand to the plow to help make those dreams come true. You walk the talk better than anyone I know. And if anyone asks me about you, all I can say is "Dis heffah heah is da truth!"

If you look up generosity in the dictionary you will see a picture of Claire Vorster. My angel, your eye is impeccable. Thank you for tolerating my Molotov cocktail of high school grammar and Ebonics to make certain that the uncrossed got crossed and that the undotted got dotted.

To the "Grand Duchess of Hand-Holding," Lisa Knight of DesignsDoneNow.com. You took my manuscript and made a masterpiece. (Sorry about the sweaty palms.)

Many Hands Make Light Work

I would like to express my gratitude to every family member, friend, fan and foe that contributed in any way to support the publication of this book. Your love and generosity is everything! I especially want to thank those who dished up a little sumpthin' sumpthin' extra special during the Indiegogo crowdfunding campaign. Your love made all the difference!

Arise Christian Center
Vanessa Bailey
Alan Barfield
Marilyn Beaubien
Yolanda Granger Bostic
Tracey Carness
Ray Chew
Melodie Cochran
Anita Arnold Cook
Adam Christing
Cecily Gibbs
Marilyn Gill
Jaynell Grayson
Vincent Griffin, Jr.
Vince Griffin
Ralph Harris
Paul Jackson Jr.

Morning Manna

Ayesha Jarnegan
Robyn Lattaker-Johnson
Cecilia C. Juarez
Wilbert McZeal
TeeJ Mercer
Naoe
Jan Shacks
Dr. Debi Smith
Laneia Smith
Robin Smith
Tiffany Thomas
Tirralan Watkins
Roy Wood Jr.

And to those who wish to remain anonymous, please know that while your name is hidden, your generosity is on full display. God bless you all!